Now and at the Hour of Our Death

Third Edition

Instructions for My Medical Treatment, Finances, and Funeral

Nihil Obstat
Rev. Mr. Daniel G. Welter, JD
Chancellor
Archdiocese of Chicago
April 18, 2022

Imprimatur
Most Rev. Robert G. Casey
Vicar General
Archdiocese of Chicago
April 18, 2022

The *Nihil Obstat* and *Imprimatur* are official declarations that a book is free of doctrinal and moral error. No implication is contained therein that those who have granted the *Nihil Obstat* and *Imprimatur* agree with the content, opinions, or statements expressed. Nor do they assume any legal responsibility associated with publication.

Excerpts from *Lectionary for Mass for Use in the Dioceses of the United States of America, Second Typical Edition* © 1998, 1997, 1970 by the Confraternity of Christian Doctrine, Inc., Washington, DC, and are reproduced herein by license of the copyright owner. All rights reserved. No part of *Lectionary for Mass* may be reproduced in any form without permission in writing from the Confraternity of Christian Doctrine, Inc., Washington, DC.

Excerpts from the English translation of the *Catechism of the Catholic Church* for use in the United States of America © 1994, United States Catholic Conference, Inc.—Libreria Editrice Vaticana. Used with permission. English translation of the *Catechism of the Catholic Church: Modifications from the Editio Typica* © 1997, United States Conference of Catholic Bishops—Libreria Editrice Vaticana.

Excerpts from the English translation of *Pastoral Care of the Sick: Rites of Anointing and Viaticum* © 1982, International Commission on English in the Liturgy Corporation (ICEL); excerpts from the English translation of *Order of Christian Funerals* © 1985, 1989, ICEL; excerpts from the English translation of *The Roman Missal* © 2010, ICEL. All rights reserved. Published with the approval of the Committee on Divine Worship, United States Conference of Catholic Bishops.

Excerpts from Vatican documents are reprinted with the kind permission of Libreria Editrice Vaticana.

This resource is based on a publication of Catholic Cemeteries in the Archdiocese of Chicago. Additional text written by Joseph DeGrocco, Mary G. Fox, Peter Gilmour, Lilivette Guzman, Timothy A. Johnston, David A. Lysik, Danielle A. Noe, Lorie Simmons, and Victoria M. Tufano.

Now and at the Hour of Our Death, Third Edition: Instructions for My Medical Treatment, Finances, and Funeral materials may not be photocopied, digitally shared, or otherwise reproduced without permission in writing from the copyright holder above, except for those pages and materials found on the accompanying website: www.LTP.org/HOUR3. Materials found on the accompanying website may be reproduced and shared digitally with family members only by the persons who purchased this resource. Materials found on the website must be reproduced along with their accompanying copyright notices. Reproduction of any other part of this resource for any other purpose is both illegal and unethical.

NOW AND AT THE HOUR OF OUR DEATH, THIRD EDITION: INSTRUCTIONS FOR MY MEDICAL TREATMENT, FINANCES, AND FUNERAL © 2022 Archdiocese of Chicago: Liturgy Training Publications, 3949 South Racine Avenue, Chicago, IL 60609; 800-933-1800, fax: 800-933-7094, email: orders@ltp.org; website: www.LTP.org. All rights reserved.

This book was edited by Danielle A. Noe. Víctor R. Pérez was the production editor, and Juan Alberto Castillo was the designer and the production artist. The original publication was designed by Peter Pona and Jim Mellody-Pizzato. The original editors were David A. Lysik and Bryan Cones.

Cover art by Diane Knott.

26 25 24 23 22   1 2 3 4 5

Printed in the United States of America

Library of Congress Control Number: 2022931046

ISBN: 978-1-61671-679-0

HOUR3

CONTENTS

A LETTER TO READERS   1

CHAPTER ONE
End-of-Life Sacramental, Medical, and Legal Information   5
    Sacramental Requests   5
    Medical Treatment and Legal Issues   6
    Advance Directives   6
    Durable Power of Attorney for Health Care   8
    Living Will   11
    Physican Orders for Life-Sustaining Treatment (POLST)   13
    Do-Not-Resuscitate Order (DNR)   14
    Mental Health Treatment Preference   15
    No Advance Directives?   15
    Donation of Organs and Body   16
    Making a Will   18
    Durable Power of Attorney for Financial Management   19

CHAPTER TWO
Finances, Policies, Subscriptions, and Other Accounts   21
    Chart of Accounts   22

CHAPTER THREE
Funeral Home Arrangements   26
    Gathering Information   27
    Prepaying for Funeral Goods and Services   27
    Funeral Consumers Alliance   29
    Cremation Society or Crematorium   29
    Preparation of the Body   30
    Personal Effects and Keepsakes   32
    Cremation   32
    The Coffin or Casket   34
    The Urn   35
    Repatriation of the Body   36

CHAPTER FOUR
Cemetery Arrangements   39
    Burial   39
    Natural Burial   42
    Private Burial   44

　　　　Memorial Marker and Inscription　44
　　　　Grave Decorations　45

CHAPTER FIVE
Obituary and Memorial Information　46
　　　　Obituary　46
　　　　Prayer or Memorial Cards　49
　　　　Memorial Requests　49
　　　　Memorial Video　50
　　　　Memorial Items　50
　　　　Social Media　51
　　　　Memorial Luncheon or Dinner　51

CHAPTER SIX
Catholic Funeral Services or Rites　52
　　　　The Vigil for the Deceased　53
　　　　　　Outline of Service　55
　　　　The Funeral Liturgy　56
　　　　　　Outlines of Services　59
　　　　The Rite of Committal　61
　　　　　　Outline of Service　62
　　　　Scripture Readings　62
　　　　Funeral Music Suggestions　65

CHAPTER SEVEN
Talking to Your Family about Death　67
　　　　Letter to Loved Ones　70

APPENDIX
Tasks for My Loved Ones　71
　　　　Prayers before Death and at the Time of Death　71
　　　　Tasks Immediately upon Death　73
　　　　Preparation of the Body　73
　　　　Transferring the Body　74
　　　　Death Certificate　74
　　　　Wake (Vigil Service), Funeral Mass, and Burial　74
　　　　Immediately after Burial　75
　　　　In the Days after Burial　75
　　　　Persons to Notify　76

A LETTER TO READERS

> Hail Mary, full of grace,
> the Lord is with you.
> Blessed are you among women,
> and blessed is the fruit of your womb, Jesus.
> Holy Mary, Mother of God,
> pray for us sinners,
> now and at the hour of our death.
> Amen.

Dear Reader,

The title of this booklet is probably quite familiar to you, as it comes from the beloved "Hail Mary" prayer. Throughout your Christian life, you have probably offered this prayer on numerous occasions while praying the Rosary, as your daily offering, or when seeking comfort. You may have prayed the "Hail Mary" upon learning that a loved one had died. But this prayer puts our *own* death at the forefront of our mind. "Pray for us *sinners now and at the hour of our death*" (emphasis added). It can be daunting to think about our own death. St. Benedict teaches us that we should "keep death always before your eyes."[1] To some this might seem depressing or even morbid. But as a Christian, death is not something to fear! When Jesus Christ was handed over to die, he counseled his followers not to fear death—neither his death nor their own. "Do not let your hearts be troubled," he said. "You have faith in God; have faith also in me."[2]

> In the face of death, the Church confidently proclaims that God has created each person for eternal life and that Jesus, the Son of God, by his Death and Resurrection, has broken the chains of sin and death that bound humanity.
>
> —*Order of Christian Funerals*, 1*

---

1. *Rule of St. Benedict*, chapter 4, paragraph 47.
2. 2 John 14:1.
* The *Order of Christian Funerals* is the book that includes all of the Catholic Church's rituals surrounding death—prayers, Scripture readings, directions for how to celebrate the rites, and theological reflections. Prayer texts from this ritual book are used throughout this resource.

Jesus' death changed everything. Jesus chose absolute obedience to God, and God raised him from the dead. By his resurrection, Christ shattered the power of sin and death over humanity revealed most fully God's desire that human beings live in eternal happiness with God. Through his death and resurrection Christ conquered death and opened the doors of heaven to an eternal relationship with God.

> In him the hope of blessed resurrection has dawned, that those saddened by the certainty of dying might be consoled by the promise of immortality to come.
> Indeed for your faithful, Lord, life is changed not ended, and, when this earthly dwelling turns to dust, an eternal dwelling is made ready for them in heaven.
>
> —Preface I for the Dead

We are participants in the resurrection, not spectators. This participation began with our baptism where we have already experienced death. At baptism, when immersed into the life-giving water, you intimately shared in Jesus' death on the cross, shedding your old self, and coming forth from the font as a new creation, sharing in Christ's resurrection. By sharing in Christ's paschal mystery (his life, death, and resurrection), we have learned—and work toward—dying to self each day so that we can fully share in the resurrection.

Bodily death is not the end, but our birth into heavenly glory. In death, "Life is changed not ended."[3] Christians believe that death is not the end of life, but the continuation of life! The life we were given at conception does not end, it is transformed. Who we are on earth is who we are in heaven, forgiven by a merciful God for our sins and made perfect by the death and resurrection of Christ.

A Gift for Loved Ones: Filling Out This Booklet

This booklet is a prayerful and practical guide. It gives you the opportunity to reflect on your wishes regarding your health care if you become unable to communicate your decisions. It asks you to think about what means you wish to be used to prolong your life and about such things as organ donation. It encourages you to prepare in advance for the management of your financial resources and for the disposition of your goods. It allows you to record the information that your survivors will need at the time of your death.

This booklet also encourages you to educate yourself about funeral services, the options that are available for a funeral, and the costs involved. It also provides you the opportunity to think about and suggest some elements of your funeral and burial liturgy. That liturgy is the Church's liturgy, the same for all the baptized regardless of wealth or attainment. But it is also intended to be a particular prayer for the individual Christian who has died.

---

3. Preface I for the Dead.

Continually return to what you have written in the pages that follow. Review and update the information as needed; your wishes might change as your journey in life. Since this booklet records personal information such as bank account numbers and your social security number, you will want to keep it in safe place until the time comes for your loved ones to access the information. If you prefer to fill out this booklet electronically, PDF files have been prepared for you and are available for download on the following website: **www.LTP.org/HOUR3**. You will need to enter this password to access the files: **$.2fGDB5**

When you prepare well for illness and death, these preparations are a genuine gift to family and friends. Preparing for your own death removes a great burden off the shoulders of loved ones who are suffering deep sadness upon your death. Preparing ahead of time will help them be able to grieve without worrying if they are fulfilling your wishes and also help them avoid conflict with other family members. This is a wonderful opportunity to have a deep conversation with family members about your beliefs and fill out this booklet together. For Christians, planning for serious illness and death is primarily an act of stewardship and a response to the act of faith begun in baptism.

> **Christian hope faces the reality of death and the anguish of grief but trusts confidently that the power of sin and death has been vanquished by the risen Lord.**
>
> —*Order of Christian Funerals*, 8

To prepare for your own death is to actively mediate upon Christ's paschal mystery—his life, death, and glorious resurrection. Though this book is about practical details, it also gives you a way to befriend death, to appreciate its reality as a way to come into the fullness of God's kingdom.

We wish you God's peace during your preparations and pray for your own peaceful death and that your own loved ones are received with God's mercy at the heavenly banquet.

—The Editors and Writers

Disclaimer: *Now and at the Hour of Our Death* is intended to introduce the reader to several areas of concern surrounding death and dying, to invite further study, and to encourage informed decision making. The information in this book is not intended to substitute for the advice of a trained, licensed health care or legal professional. Readers should consult their physicians and therapists on questions of health care, and their attorneys for advice on legal matters.

On the Cover

A dogwood flower graces the cover of this booklet.
Legend tells us that the wood of the dogwood tree was
used for the wood of the cross; however, with its
beautiful white flowers forming the shape of the cross,
the dogwood has been used throughout Christianity
as a symbol of death and eternal life.
It is often used for decoration during Easter Time.

 CHAPTER ONE

End-of-Life Sacramental, Medical, and Legal Information

> The dignity of this life is linked not only to its beginning, to the fact that it comes from God, but also to its final end, to its destiny of fellowship with God in knowledge and love of him.
> —*Evangelium vitae*, 38

Sacramental Requests

The Church wishes to accompany the dying Christian with prayer. The greatest expression of this is viaticum: holy Communion received by the Christian when in danger of death. When you are ill or in danger of death, a priest, deacon, or lay minister should be called to visit you, to pray with you, and to give you holy Communion. The anointing of the sick may be administered only by a priest at any time you are ill or when the time of your death is near. The priest will also be able to celebrate the sacrament of reconciliation with you. If you are in the hospital, the hospital chaplain will be able to help your family members call a priest or lay minister. If you are homebound, be sure to contact your parish directly. They will be able to send a priest or lay minister to your home.

☐ I would like to receive the sacraments when I am ill or in a hospital or homebound.

☐ I would like to receive the sacraments when the time of my death is near.

Name of Parish: _____

Name of Priest: _____

Name of Lay Minister of Care: _____

Address: _____

_____

Telephone: _____

Email/website: _____

Medical Treatment and Legal Issues

We live in a complex society, and the legalities surrounding illness and death may seem cumbersome. Leaving a will and furnishing information about insurance and death benefits is a great kindness to your survivors. The time and expense involved need not be great.

Medical knowledge now makes it possible to prolong life to an extent that, in individual cases, may be neither necessary nor wise nor compassionate. Legal concerns also surround medical practices. When the time comes for decisions, you may be incapable of communicating your own wishes regarding prolonged treatment. That is why many people now give clear direction to both medical personnel and family members regarding their wishes about prolonging life through legal documents known as advance directives.

Advances in medicine also make it possible for people to donate their organs for specific uses or their bodies for medical research. Such decisions should be made well in advance of death.

Family members should be informed of decisions regarding life-prolonging medical treatment and donation of organs or of the body. Cards indicating execution of an advance directive or such decisions organ donation may be carried; your state may allow organ donor status to be indicated on a driver's license.[1]

Advance Directives

As a competent adult, you have the right to make decisions about your health care, and this right is not extinguished or lost when you become unable to make your own decisions. You have the right to execute "advance directives," written and legally recognized statements directing medical treatment decision making when you can no longer make them for yourself. Federal law requires that when you are admitted to a health care facility you are to be informed of your right to make advance directives. Hospitals in your area will likely have printed information available regarding

---

1. Ethics surrounding health care and end of life issues can be confusing. The United States Conference of Catholic Bishops provides the *Ethical and Religious Directives for Catholic Health Care Services*. Now in its sixth edition, it may be found online: https://www.usccb.org/about/doctrine/ethical-and-religious-directives/upload/ethical-religious-directives-catholic-health-service-sixth-edition-2016-06.pdf. All websites that are referenced in this booklet can be accessed online with the "Resources" PDF found here: www.LTP.org/HOUR3. This file has been provided for your personal research.

advance directives in general. The Catholic Health Association of the United States also produces general material on advance directives: www.chausa.org.

Three of the most commonly used advance directives are the durable power of attorney for health care (see page 8), the living will (see page 11), and POLST (see page 13). In addition, some states have recognized mental health treatment preference declarations.

When drafting your power of attorney for health care and your living will, you will need to know your preferences regarding the provision of life-sustaining treatments. Catholic moral teaching allows for the discontinuation of medical treatments that are "burdensome, dangerous, extraordinary, or disproportionate to the expected outcome,"[2] as long as the ordinary or normal care due to a sick person in similar cases continues uninterrupted.[3] You might find it helpful to discuss the moral issues surrounding medical care, death, and dying with your pastor or another minister. More information is available from the Catholic Health Association of the United States (www.chausa.org) and the United States Conference of Catholic Bishops (https://www.usccb.org/committees/pro-life-activities advance-medical-directives-planning-your-future).

It is entirely your right to choose whether to execute any advance directive, but regardless of your decision, consider the value of at least discussing your wishes regarding your health care with family members or close personal friends, as appropriate. Consider also communicating your wishes to your physician, and taking an active and informed role in choosing treatment options and designing a health care plan.

> **MORAL GUIDANCE**
>
> When we think about end-of-life decisions, there are three basic Catholic beliefs:
>
> 1. Each one of us has been created in the image and likeness of God. We are called to protect human life and be good stewards of this gift.
>
> 2. Stewardship of life should avoid the opposite extremes of the deliberate hastening of death and the overzealous use of medical treatment to extend life artificially and prolong the dying process.
>
> 3. The suffering that comes from illness and death is a way of being deeply united with the death and resurrection of Our Lord, Jesus Christ. Death is not the end; it is the doorway to eternal life.[4]

If you do choose to execute one or more advance directives, be aware that such directives do little on their own. The agent and any successor agent you name in a power of attorney should likewise know of your wishes and be given a copy. Your physician should know of their existence and should be provided with a copy. Advance directives that are signed and then put in a safe-deposit box and

---

2. *Catechism of the Catholic Church*, 2278.
3. See *Catechism of the Catholic Church*, 2279.
4. "POLST Q&A" as provided by the Catholic Health Association of the United States; available here: https://www.chausa.org/publications/health-care-ethics-usa/archives/issues/summer-2013/polst-q-a. For more information about POLST visit the following website: https://www.chausa.org/publications/health-care-ethics-usa/article/fall-2010/polst https://polst.org/.

never discussed or distributed are worthless. Think of advance directives as more than an end in themselves. Use them as opportunities for communication with your physician and with other people you consider important to your health care decision- making. The real value of executing advance directives lies more in their potential to encourage honest communication with your health care providers and loved ones, and your informed participation in decisions affecting your health care, than in simply completing legal formalities.

Durable Power of Attorney for Health Care

The document known as the durable power of attorney for health care allows you to designate a person (your "agent") to whom you give the power to make health care decisions for you, consistent with your wishes and values, in the event you become incompetent. The powers you give to your agent may be as broad or as narrow as you wish and specified in the document.

Almost every state has enacted legislation that authorizes durable powers of attorney for health care, and most state statutes include a standard form of the document, which is often made available at hospitals, nursing homes, pharmacies, office supply stores, senior centers, bar associations, the offices of health care professionals, and online. These forms should be completed thoughtfully and carefully, and you may need to consult with medical professionals and clergy when it comes to formulating specific treatment directives. Standard forms for each state are available for free from www.rocketlawyer.com. Legally valid advance directive forms which are formulated in accord with Catholic moral teaching are available state by state at www.catholicendoflife.org. Such forms may also be available from your diocesan health care office or respect life office.

The standard form generally gives your agent broad powers to make any and all health care decisions for you, including the authority to select a health care provider; admit or discharge you from any hospital; visit you in the hospital under the same right granted to a spouse,* or adult child; obtain access to your medical records and consent to their release; require, consent to, or withdraw any type of medical treatment, including whether to withdraw artificially assisted nutrition and hydration and other life-sustaining measures; and make a disposition of your body for medical purposes, authorize an autopsy, and direct the disposition of your remains.

Whether you use a standard form or create your own, following the requirements of the applicable state law, you may limit any power you give your agent, or you may give only specific powers, in accord with the law of your state. In addition to naming your agent, your durable power of attorney for health care may provide the opportunity to state your wishes regarding particular medical treatments (such as surgery,

---

*In the United States, a domestic partner may be legally chosen as power of attorney. Its mention here is meant to reflect civil law and not Church teaching.

cardiopulmonary resuscitation, ventilation, intubation, medically assisted nutrition and hydration [tube feeding], blood transfusion, chemotherapy, medication, amputation). You also may specify your wishes regarding what measures should or should not be taken in the event you have a terminal illness and have become unable to communicate your wishes. In making your choices, you need adequate medical information, and you might need to consult with your health care providers. You should also make sure that your wishes are in accord with Catholic moral teaching.

> Ordinary means are forms of treatment or care that in the judgment of the patient offer a reasonable hope of benefit and do not entail an excessive burden or impose excessive expense on the family or the community. Out of deep respect for the gift of life, we must always accept, and others must provide, ordinary means of preserving life. Ordinary means of medical care are morally obligatory.

> But Catholics are not bound to prolong the dying process by using every medical treatment available. Allowing natural death to occur is not the same as killing a patient. Some forms of medical treatment may be considered "extraordinary"—those that in the patient's judgment do not offer a reasonable hope of benefit or that entail an excessive burden or impose excessive expense on the family or the community. Catholics are not morally bound to use "extraordinary means" of medical care.[5]

> You may designate a successor agent (or successor agents, although only one may act in your name at any time) to act if the named agent is unable, unwilling, or unavailable to serve when needed. No agent is under any duty to act or to exercise any power you have given them simply because they are named as your agent, and it is helpful to name a successor agent.

> In some states, you must at least inform your physician of the existence of your durable power of attorney for health care. In any case, you should discuss the contents of your power of attorney with your physician, your agent, and your successor agent and to provide each of them with a photocopy of your completed form.

> In many cases you will also find it beneficial to discuss your wishes and the contents of your power of attorney with others as well, such as close friends and family members.

> ☐ I have discussed my wishes regarding my medical care with my agent, and any successor agent, and have provided them with a copy of my durable power of attorney for health care.

> ☐ I have executed a durable power of attorney for health care.

---

[5]. Prepared by the Diocese of Manchester, New Hampshire, and printed in *Catholic Citizenship News Education Bulletin* as found here: https://www.catholicnh.org/assets/Documents/Community/Current-Issues/CCN-CareEndofLife.pdf. Used with permission.

The original form is kept:_____

My named agent is

    Name:_____

    Address:_____

    _____

    Telephone: _____

    Email/website: _____

☐ I have named a successor agent. My successor agent is

    Name: _____

    Address: _____

    _____

    Telephone: _____

    Email/website:_____

☐ I have informed my physician of the existence and contents of my durable power of attorney for health care, and have provided a copy to my physician's office for inclusion in my medical records.

    Name of physician: _____

    Name of clinic:_____

    Address: _____

    _____

    Telephone: _____

    Email/website:_____

☐ I have not executed a durable power of attorney for health care.

☐ I have researched or made arrangements with a retirement community, an assisted living facility, or a nursing home.

    Name of community:_____

    Contact person:_____

    Address: _____

    _____

    Telephone: _____

    Email/website:_____

☐ I have researched or made arrangements with a home care organization.

Name of organization: _____

Contact person: _____

Address: _____

_____

Telephone: _____

Email/website: _____

Living Will

The living will is a document in which you make a declaration of your health care wishes in the event that you have a terminal illness or irreversible condition that will result in death in a relatively short period of time and are unable to communicate your health care decisions. Depending on the state, a living will document may also include a state of permanent unconsciousness (a persistent vegetative state). A living will directs that life-prolonging medical procedures not be used in these circumstances. Procedures that ease pain and those that maintain the comfort and dignity of the person will still be provided.

Most states have enacted legislation recognizing living wills, and many of these state laws provide simple forms that you may use to create your own living will. Usually, in addition to bearing your own signature, living wills must be witnessed by two individuals eighteen years of age or older who are not related to you by blood or marriage, not entitled to inherit from you, not financially responsible for your health care, and not your physician. Under most living will laws, one or two physicians must certify, in writing, that the patient meets the conditions for the living will to go into effect. It is important that you follow your state's regulations for living wills, as some requirements vary from state to state, such as the need for the living will to be notarized or periodically renewed. AARP provides the forms for each state for free: https://www.aarp.org/caregiving/financial-legal/free-printable-advance-directives/. This Catholic website also provides legally valid end of life forms organized by state: www.catholicendoflife.org.

As with the durable power of attorney for health care, it is most helpful to provide your physician with a copy of your living will well in advance of any immediate need. In most cases, it is also beneficial to give copies to your family members and close friends, and to discuss its contents with them. The original should be kept in a secure, but known and easily accessible place.

It is important to remember that by its nature the living will deals only with your wishes to discontinue life-prolonging medical procedures in a limited range of circumstances. So, while the living will provides some benefit, it is wise to also have a durable power of attorney for health care that names your agent for the purpose of making all health care decisions (including routine, day-to-day decisions) on your behalf when you are incompetent to do so, even if you are not necessarily terminally ill.

The Catholic Church teaches that all life is sacred from conception until natural death. The medical treatments, decisions, and advanced directives that we make should uphold Catholic values and moral principles. Even if you have a living will, you should still select a friend, family member, or doctor who shares your Catholic beliefs and would be able to safeguard and protect your values. You are encouraged to talk through these important life decisions with a designated person.

> A living will, . . . simply lists treatment options or care that the patient wishes to accept or reject. No matter how well-crafted, such a document can never predict all the possible problems that may occur at a later time or anticipate all future treatment options. A living will can be misinterpreted by medical providers who might not understand the patient's wishes.[6]

This is another reason to supplement a living will with a durable power of attorney for health care document which provides for an individual to represent you in discussions with health care providers.

☐ I have executed a living will.

The original form is kept:_____

_____

☐ I have informed my physician of the existence and contents of my living will, and I have provided a copy to my physician's office for inclusion in my medical records. (See page 10 for physician's information.)

☐ I have provided a copy of my living will to the hospital where I would likely be taken for care.

Name of hospital: _____

Address: _____

_____

Telephone: _____

Email/website: _____

☐ I have informed my family members of the existence and contents of my living will, and I have provided at least one family member or close personal friend with a copy of my living will.

Name of person: _____

---

[6]. "Advance Medical Directives: Planning for Your Future" available from the USCCB; https://www.usccb.org/committees/pro-life-activities/advance-medical-directives-planning-your-future.

Address: _____

Telephone: _____

Email: _____

☐ I have not executed a living will; however, I would like Catholic teaching to guide my loved ones decisions about end of life treatment.

Physican Orders for Life-Sustaining Treatment (POLST)

The Physician Orders for Life-Sustaining Treatment (POLST) is an order from a physician that addresses end-of-life decision-making. This form is usually prepared when a person has a terminal illness, is very frail, or is hospitalized. The physician will fill out and sign this order after speaking to the patient about his or her wishes. The POLST form provides information such as specific medical treatments and care plans you would like or whether CPR should be administered. It is much more detailed than a DNR and "gives seriously ill or frail people more specific direction over their health care treatments compared to advance directives."[7] The form is easily accessible by various providers and facilities; it is found in the patient's medical record.

POLST is not permanent and can be voided (each state has a different process for voiding a POLST form). Although these are medical orders, the doctor must sign the form; the patient may do so if it is within their capabilities to do so. Once ordered and signed, it immediately takes effect.

> POLST is not just a specific set of medical orders documented on a form; it is also an approach to end-of-life planning based on conversations between patients, loved ones, and medical professionals. The POLST Paradigm is designed to ensure that seriously ill patients can choose the treatments they want and that their wishes are honored by medical providers.
>
> A key component of the system is thoughtful, facilitated advance care planning conversations between health care professionals and patients and those close to them. Completion of a POLST form requires shared decision making between the health care professional signing the form and the patient, or his/her legally authorized health care representative identified pursuant to state law. In order to complete the POLST form, there must be a discussion of the patient's diagnosis and prognosis; the available treatment options given the current circumstances, including the benefits and burdens of those treatments; and the patient's goals of care and preferences of treatment. Together they reach an informed decision about

---

7. "Honoring the Wishes of Those with Serious Illness and Frailty" as provided by National POLST; available here: https://polst.org/.

desired treatment, based on the person's values, beliefs and goals for care. Then, if they wish, their health care professional completes and signs a POLST form based on the patient's expressed treatment references.[8]

Not every state has approved POLST for patient use. Consult with your doctor to see if this is an option for you. Patients should be aware that a POLST form does not take the place of an advanced directive. "While all competent adults—regardless of health status—should have an advance directive, not everyone should have a POLST. As discussed above, POLST is for a very specific patient population. The POLST form is a set of medical orders, similar to the resuscitate (allow natural death) order. POLST is not an advance directive. POLST does not substitute for naming a health care agent or durable power of attorney for health care."[9]

- ☐ I have spoken to my doctor about POLST. (See page 10 for physician's information.)
- ☐ A POLST form can be found in my medical records.
- ☐ POLST is not an option in my state.
- ☐ I have not made any arrangements about POLST.

Do-Not-Resuscitate Order (DNR)

A do-not-resuscitate order, or DNR, is not the same as a living will or a durable power of attorney for health care. A DNR is a written instruction or signed form from your physician directing health care works providers to refrain from resuscitating a patient if the person has no pulse and is not breathing. Resuscitation could involve mouth-to-mouth, chest compressions, machine breathing, defibrillators, or medicine. A DNR is the patient's choice done in careful consultation with the physician. Decisions about a DNR order should be based on the potential benefits and burdens of resuscitation for the particular patient.

- ☐ I have a DNR order and it is found in my medical records. (See page 10 for physician's information.)
- ☐ I do not have a DNR order; but these are my wishes:

_____

_____

---

8. "POLST Q&A" as provided by the Catholic Health Association of the United States; available here: https://www.chausa.org/publications/health-care-ethics-usa/archives/issues/summer-2013/polst-q-a. Additional helpful information is found on this website. Used with permission from the Catholic Health Association (CHA).

9. "POLST Q&A" as provided by the Catholic Health Association of the United States; available here: https://www.chausa.org/publications/health-care-ethics-usa/archives/issues/summer-2013/polst-q-a. For more information about POLST visit the following website: https://www.chausa.org/publications/health-care-ethics-usa/article /fall-2010/polst https://polst.org/.

Mental Health Treatment Preference

When thinking about your health care advance directives, it is important to consider your mental health, as well as any particular concerns you may have. It is also important to learn of your state's laws in this regard. In some states the agent named in a Durable Power of Attorney for Health Care document is generically given the power to make decisions regarding mental health treatment, subject to specific directives given by the person executing the document. On the other hand, there are some states in which the advance directive limits the decisions that may be made about mental health care and may prohibit your agent from making mental health treatment decisions. Yet other states have established a freestanding psychiatric advance directive in which a person can indicate his or her wishes regarding admission to a mental health treatment facility and regarding such treatments as psychotropic medications, electroconvulsive therapy, restraint and seclusion. This document may also allow you to appoint an agent for mental health treatment decisions. The National Resource Center on Psychiatric Advance Directives provides information for each state: www.ncr-pad.org/states/.[10]

- ☐ I have learned of my state's laws regarding advance directives and mental health care.
- ☐ I have thought about my wishes concerning my mental health treatment, and I have taken the necessary steps (following my state's laws) to make my wishes known to my healthcare agent and to my physician. (See page 10 for physician information.)

Name of Mental Health Therapist/Physician: _____

_____

Name of clinic: _____

Address: _____

_____

Telephone: _____

Email/website: _____

No Advance Directives?

You have the right not to execute any advance directives regarding your medical treatment in the event you are no longer able to communicate your wishes. But if you have not executed an advance directive, decisions regarding your health care

---

10. Prepared by the Diocese of Manchester, New Hampshire, and printed in *Catholic Citizenship News Education Bulletin* as found here: https://www.catholicnh.org/assets/Documents/Community/Current-Issues/CCN-CareEndofLife.pdf. Used with permission.

will have to be made by someone else—someone who might not be the person you would have chosen.

The laws of many states provide that if you are not able to make your own health care decisions, and in the absence of an advance directive, a "health care surrogate" or "proxy" may be chosen to make your health care decisions for you. Typically, there is a prioritized list of proxy decision makers which may include such individuals as a court appointed guardian, your spouse, an adult child, a parent, an adult brother or sister. Some lists include other adult relatives (a grandparent, adult grandchild, nieces and nephews, aunts and uncles) and a close friend. Some states insert other people in various positions of priority into this basic listing (for example, a member of the clergy known to you*). Your state's law should be consulted for information about the prioritized list of proxy decision makers that is used.

The chosen surrogate or proxy is to make health care decisions for you based on whatever he or she knows of your wishes; otherwise, the surrogate is to make decisions in accord with his or her determination of your best interests. If you choose not to execute any advance directive, you should discuss your thoughts and desires regarding your health care, as well as some of your personal, philosophical, religious, or moral beliefs, with those people most likely to be chosen to act as your health care surrogate.

- ☐ I have chosen not to execute any advance directive regarding my health care.
- ☐ Here are my wishes concerning my medical treatment in the event I become incompetent to communicate my desires:

  _____
  _____

- ☐ Catholic teaching is important to me and should be considered by my proxy or surrogate.
- ☐ I have spoken of my wishes with the following candidates likely to be chosen to act as my health care surrogate or proxy (add names here):

  _____
  _____

Donation of Organs and Body

Some people choose to donate their usable organs to "organ banks" or their bodies for medical research. Catholic tradition supports such decisions. The *Catechism of the Catholic Church* states:

---

*State laws concerning a health proxy may vary. Some states will allow a long-term domestic partner be a health proxy. Its inclusion here is meant to reflect the possible differences from state to state and not Church teaching.

Organ transplants are in conformity with the moral law if the physical and psychological dangers and risks to the donor are proportionate to the good sought for the recipient. Organ donation after death is a noble and meritorious act and is to be encouraged as an expression of generous solidarity. It is not morally acceptable if the donor or his proxy has not given explicit consent. Moreover, it is not morally admissible to bring about the disabling mutilation or death of a human being, even in order to delay the death of other persons.[11]

Autopsies can be morally permitted for legal inquests or scientific research. The free gift of organs after death is legitimate and can be meritorious.[12]

Arrangements for organ donations and donation of the body should be made in advance. When death occurs, time is of the essence for useful donation of organs. Organs may only be retrieved when the person has been declared dead according to accepted medical criteria (dead donor rule). A donor card, which can be carried in one's wallet, aids in fulfilling your wishes in this regard. Many states now have a place on the back of a driver's license where one can indicate specific organs or the entire body for donation.

It is important to discuss these intentions with family members, friends, and if applicable, the person you named as your agent in your power of attorney for health care. Even though a donor card has been signed, doctors usually will not remove organs without the consent of the family or health care agent. Information about becoming an organ donor can be found here: www.organdonor.gov. Information about donating your body to science can be found here: www.sciencecare.co.

☐ I am not an organ donor.

☐ I am an organ donor.

☐ I have made the following arrangements for donating my body to science:

_____

_____

_____

The Catholic Church requires that bodies or cremated remains be buried following the removal of organs or after scientific research on your body has concluded. (Refer to chapter 4.)

---

11. *Catechism of the Catholic Church*, 2296.
12. *Catechism of the Catholic Church*, 2301.

Making a Will

A will is a legal document, usually drawn up by a lawyer and witnessed by at least two people. If you care about how your financial and material assets will be distributed after your death, you need a will. Even if you consider yourself to be of modest financial means, or if you have set up certain direct beneficiary transfers (contracts such as life insurance policies, IRAs, trust accounts, and so on, where the assets are distributed apart from a will) or a living trust, it is a good idea to consider making a will.

A will lets you control how your estate will be distributed, and thus gives you the opportunity to make the best arrangements for those you care about. In your will you can also name a guardian for young children and for adult children with special needs. Although a third party can contest the choice of a guardian named in a will, courts do usually presume that the person named in the parent's will is the best choice for taking care of the children. If guardianship is not established, a court will appoint a guardian, which is usually a family member. If there are no family members or others willing to become the guardian, children will become wards of the state and may end up in foster care. You should also designate a caregiver for pets and farm animals; otherwise they could be placed in a shelter, mistreated, or euthanized. If you die intestate (that is, without a will), any property that has not been distributed by other means will be distributed according to state intestacy laws, under which only spouses,* and blood relatives may inherit; friends and charities may not inherit under state intestacy laws.

While individuals with large estates should definitely consult an attorney when preparing a will, it is prudent for anyone considering a will to work with an attorney. In many larger cities, local bar associations sponsor programs that offer no- or low-cost will-related consultation with an attorney and low-cost preparation of a simple will. In addition, bar associations also provide lawyer referral services. Computer software is available for you to create your own will (such as Quicken WillMaker & Trust) and as well as online services, some at cost and others free (such as www.rocketlawyer.com).

In your will you will need to appoint an executor—a person responsible for carrying out the directions in your will. This person should be someone who is trustworthy, competent to handle financial matters, able to communicate clearly, and someone with whom you feel close enough to share a wide range of personal facts. In some situations, it might be beneficial to discuss the appointment of your executor with your family members. Depending on your circumstances, instead of naming a family member or friend to serve as executor, you might want to consider naming a corporate executor, such as an authorized bank or trust company. Refer to https://executor.org for information about selecting and acting as an executor.

---

*Inheritance laws for domestic partners will vary from state to state. Its mention here is meant to reflect the possible differences from state to state and not Church teaching.

☐ I have made a will.

    My will is kept:_____

    Person (or software/website) who prepared my will:_____

    _____

    Witnesses of my will: _____

    Executor named in my will: _____

    Person I have named as guardian of minor children (if applicable): _____

    _____

    Person I have named as guardian of my adult children with special needs (if applicable): _____

    Person I have named as guardian of my animals (if applicable):_____

    _____

☐ I have not made a will.

Durable Power of Attorney for Financial Management

Planning in advance for the management of financial resources in the event of a serious illness is an important consideration that everyone faces. The document, known as a durable power of attorney for financial management, allows you to designate another person or persons or authorized bank or trust company (your *agent*) to manage your financial affairs during your lifetime in the event you are unable to do so. (The term *durable* means that the document continues in effect even after you become incapacitated.) As with the durable power of attorney for health care (see pages 9–11), you decide exactly how much authority to give to your agent.

    Typically, most people give their agent a wide range of powers so that the agent may do things like pay bills, cash checks, make bank deposits and withdrawals, and access safe-deposit boxes; or you may limit your agent's authority to one or two tasks. While most durable powers of attorney for financial management take effect immediately after they are signed and continue in force indefinitely, you may limit their effective dates as you see fit.

    You may either consult a lawyer or prepare your own durable power of attorney for financial management. Some state statutes include a model form of the document that you may easily adapt to meet your own needs, and commercial forms of this document are generally available in places like office supply and drug stores. You should be aware, however, that while your duly executed power of attorney must be honored, several banks and other financial institutions will prefer that you also complete their preprinted power of attorney form if your agent is to handle transactions on your behalf with that particular bank. To avoid problems, it is wise to check with each financial institution where you have an account and learn of their preferences. (Refer to chapter 2 regarding financial matters.)

- ☐ I have considered whether I need a durable power of attorney for financial management.
- ☐ I have executed a durable power of attorney for financial management.

    My named agent is: _____

    Address: _____

    _____

    Telephone: _____

    Email/website: _____

- ☐ I have checked with the financial institutions where I have accounts, and have filled out any required forms.
- ☐ I have decided not to execute a durable power of attorney for financial management.

    Add additional end-of-life requests here: _____

    _____
    _____
    _____
    _____
    _____
    _____
    _____
    _____
    _____
    _____
    _____
    _____

 CHAPTER TWO

Finances, Policies, Subscriptions, and Other Accounts

> As each one has received a gift, use it to serve one another
> as good stewards of God's varied grace.
> —1 Peter 4:10

Stewardship is an attitude of responsibility to God and to one another for the material goods at our disposal. Such stewardship should be our perspective in approaching the following material. Regardless of how few or how many are our possessions, we have a responsibility to use these goods wisely. The careful answering of the items on the following pages is an exercise in stewardship.

Keep in mind that by filling out this form, you will be entering personal information such as your social security number, account numbers, and passwords. You will want to keep this booklet in a very safe place and where no one will be able to access the information until the time is necessary (you want to avoid financial theft and identity theft). It would also be better if you fill this out with pencil or erasable pen since numbers and passwords are often changed and updated. This form also includes expenditures that loved ones will need to cancel (they will need copies of the death certificate and your social security number). Additional lines have been provided for you to add additional items not noted on this form. An online version of this form is available here www.LTP.org/HOUR3 (the password for this website is found in this book on page 3). If you do not wish to write your passwords and login information below or on the electronic form, there are apps you can download on your phone that store all your passwords, such as LastPass.

	Company Name	Contact Person	Phone Number	Amount Due (Paid Out or to Be Received/Balance)
Insurance, Benefits, and Retirement				
Home Owners Insurance				
Renters Insurance				
Car Insurance				
Life Insurance Policy #1				
Life Insurance Policy #2				
Credit Union Insurance				
Annuities				
IRAs				
Union Benefits				
Social Security Benefits				
Veterans Benefits				
Retirement #1				
Retirement #2				
Financial Information				
Retirement Fund				
Savings Account				
Checking Account				
Other Bank/Credit Union Account				
Mutual Funds				
Stocks				
Bonds				
Credit Card #1				
Credit Card #2				
Credit Card #3				
Credit Card #4				
Credit Card #5				
Student Loan Company				
Mortgage #1				
Mortgage #2				
HOA				
Housing Rent				
Car Loan				
Car Registration				

Website	Account Number/ Box Number	User ID/Password/ Security Question	Location of Certificate/ Deeds/Titles/Keys

	Company Name	Contact Person	Phone Number	Amount Due (Paid Out or to Be Received/Balance)
Medical Insurance				
Health Insurance				
Dental Insurance				
Vision Insurance				
Prescription Shipments				
Medicare				
Medicaid				
Home Services and Subscriptions				
House Maintenance Packages				
Water				
Gas				
Electric				
Home Services (Home Care, Landscaping, etc.)				
Cell Phone				
Landline				
Cable/TV				
Internet				
Miscellaneous				
Organizations/Clubs/Memberships				
Post Office Box				
Safety Deposit Box				
Social Security Number				
Computer				

Other accounts or subscriptions may be added below:

Website	Account Number/ Box Number	User ID/Password/ Security Question	Location of Certificate/ Deeds/Titles/Keys

 CHAPTER THREE

Funeral Home Arrangements

*The celebration of the Christian funeral brings
hope and consolation to the living.*
—*Order of Christian Funerals*, 7

If the services of a funeral home are to be employed, some planning can be done in advance.[1] If you have made no advance plans, your survivors will need to tend to a variety of things—making choices about burial, entombment and cremation, selecting the coffin or casket, or a vessel for cremated remains, deciding questions of embalming and visitation, and dealing with costs and financial concerns—often without adequate time and while simultaneously dealing with the range of emotions that accompany a death. Your survivors will also need to arrange with the parish church the time of the visitation (also called a wake or viewing), the funeral liturgy, and the committal at the cemetery. Finally, they will need to notify others of your death, and make a decision regarding the presence and content of an obituary notice in the newspapers. The staff of the funeral home will be able to ease the burden and help with these decisions.

The vast majority of people in the United States choose a funeral home to assist them at the time of death. Two practical considerations should guide you in the choice of a funeral home. The first is its reputation. Are people who have used a specific funeral home willing to recommend it? The second is cost. Use the following information to guide you in your efforts to make good decisions about planning for your funeral.

---

1. If you are planning to have Catholic services, the parish church is responsible for working with you to prepare those services. This includes the wake service if that takes place in the funeral home. Refer to chapter 6 for information about the Catholic funeral rites.

Gathering Information

You should first be aware that when you arrange for a funeral you have the option of purchasing a package of services and merchandise, or of buying individual items and services to meet your own needs. You need only select and pay for those goods and services that you want.

A federal regulation known as the Funeral Rule, enacted by the Federal Trade Commission (FTC), requires funeral homes (but not cemeteries) to provide you with certain information, whether you shop by phone or in person. Under the Funeral Rule, if you contact a funeral home by telephone and ask about funeral arrangements you must be given the prices of the services you ask about. If you contact a funeral home in person, you must be given a written copy of an itemized price list that gives the cost of each service offered by the funeral home. The Funeral Rule also requires the funeral home to provide written price lists for coffins or caskets and for outer burial containers (vaults or grave liners).

Use the Funeral Rule to help you gather information about your options for funeral and burial arrangements. Consider visiting at least two or three funeral homes (perhaps with a spouse or friend) to obtain their price lists for services, caskets or coffins, and outer burial containers. Often a parish community will work regularly with a specific funeral home. Connect with your parish to see if they can recommend funeral services. More detailed information about the Funeral Rule may be found on the Federal Trade Commission website (https://www.ftc.gov/).

Comparing lists of services and merchandise you think you would want will give you an idea of how much your funeral might cost. You can use these lists to help form your own preferences. They might also help you rethink your wishes in light of the costs. Use this information to prepare a brief statement about what you consider to be important features of your funeral and burial (disposition or internment).

Prepaying for Funeral Goods and Services

Learning about funeral costs in advance of your death can also help you begin to form plans to meet those costs. The average funeral without cremation in 2021 ranged between $7,000 and $12,000. The average cost of a funeral with cremation ranged between $6,000 to $7,000.[2] There are basic services that funeral homes provide—for example, direct burial without visitation. The more services you select, the higher the fee, which will vary by state. Social security provides some monetary assistance (a lump sum of $255.00), as do life insurance policies (you should be aware of what options will be provided to you.) The benefit of prepaying for funeral goods

---

2. Statistics provided by the Lincoln Heritage Life Insurance Company, as found at https://www.lhlic.com/consumer-resources/average-funeral-cost/. Their website provides good information regarding individual cost breakdowns.

and services is that prices can be locked in. This includes prepaying for cemetery plots (see chapter 4).

In the event that you decide to prepay for your funeral arrangements, do so with your eyes open, and be sure to ask many questions before agreeing to any contract. Clear up any misunderstandings before paying, and be sure to receive a written description of what goods and services are included. State laws vary regarding the handling of the money you prepay, and you should learn your state's law if you are prepaying.

You should also consider the location of your funeral and final resting place. Perhaps where you currently live is not the place you would like your funeral and burial to take place. Your body might need to be transported to another state or even to another country, and you may do so by car, train, or plane. This will require additional expenses, and it's likely you will need to make arrangements with a funeral home where you live as well as where you would like your funeral and burial to occur. You should be aware that you can't arrange for air transport without the assistance of a funeral home, and costs for transport can range from $1,500 to $15,000 dollars.[3] States and countries will also have varying rules for embalming and refrigeration (see also page 36).

As your plans begin to take shape, be sure to let your family members and loved ones know of your decisions. Keep copies of any paperwork in a place that is secure yet will be readily accessible to your survivors. Use what you learn about your options for funeral services and goods to make choices and plans that reflect your values and your faith.

☐ I have set up a funeral savings account at the following bank.

Name of bank: _____

Address: _____

_____

Telephone: _____

Website: _____

Account number: _____

Payable to _____

☐ I have decided not to set up a funeral savings account.

☐ I have prepaid for funeral arrangements with this funeral home.

Name: _____

Contact person: _____

---

3. "Shipping a Dead Body: 10 Things You Need to Know," FuneralWise, accessed December 9, 2021, www.funeralwise.com/2019/01/16/shipping-a-dead-body-10-things-you-need-to-know/. Refer to this website for additional information regarding the transport of a body across state and country lines.

Address: _____

_____

Telephone: _____

Email/website: _____

The contract is kept: _____

☐ I have decided not to prepay for funeral arrangements; however, I suggest the following funeral home.

Name: _____

Contact person: _____

Address: _____

_____

Telephone: _____

Email/website: _____

☐ My life insurance policy will cover funeral expenses.

Name of insurance company: _____

Contact person: _____

Telephone: _____

Plan number: _____

Amount of coverage: _____

Funeral Consumers Alliance

The goal of the Funeral Consumers Alliance is to ensure that consumers are fully prepared and protected when planning a funeral for themselves or their loved ones. They do this by offering objective facts about funeral planning so families can plan a meaningful goodbye that fits their needs and their budget. For more information visit: www.funerals.org/.

Cremation Society or Crematorium

Cremation societies or a crematorium will properly care for your loved ones and provide you with opportunities for visiting the body, services in their facility, and burial. Like a funeral home, they will offer you various packages. They would prepare the body for viewing, but would not embalm, because of cremation. A cremation society accepts memberships; a crematorium usually does not. (See pages 32–34 for more information about cremation.)

☐ I want to be cremated.

☐ I do not want to be cremated.

☐ I have a membership in the following cremation society.

Name: _____

Contact person: _____

Address: _____

_____

Telephone: _____

Email/website: _____

Specific arrangements of my membership: _____

_____

_____

_____

☐ I don't have a membership in a cremation society, but I would like my family to use a crematorium rather than a funeral home. Here is the facility I would like you to use.

Name: _____

Contact person: _____

Address: _____

_____

Telephone: _____

Email/website: _____

Preparation of the Body

Even in death, our bodies have dignity and should be prepared for burial with loving kindness and compassion. These words from the Church's ritual book for celebrating funerals may help guide the various decisions to be made about preparation of the body:

> Since in Baptism the body was marked with the seal of the Trinity and became the temple of the Holy Spirit, Christians respect and honor the bodies of the dead and the places where they rest. Any customs associated with the preparation of the body of the deceased should always be marked with dignity and reverence and never with the despair of those who have no hope. Preparation of the body should include prayer, especially at those intimate moments reserved for family members. For the final disposition of the body, it is the ancient Christian custom to bury or entomb the bodies

of the dead; cremation is permitted, unless it is evident that cremation was chosen for anti-Christian motives.[4]

A deceased person's body must be prepared for viewing, funeral services, and burial. This includes the washing and clothing of the body, the grooming of hair and nails, and makeup. If the person's appearance has been affected by trauma, accidents, or illness, "wax, adhesive and paster [is used] to recreate natural form."[5] Preparing the body includes embalming. Be sure to check with the laws of your state concerning the preparation of the body. Most people are not aware that embalming is not legally required if the body is buried quickly. The timing will vary from state to state, but it is usually within 48 to 72 hours. Coordination will be required among the family, the funeral home or crematorium, and the parish church. If the environment is a concern to you, know that the burial of your body is the more natural and ecological choice.

In countries or regions where a funeral professional, and not the family or community, carries out the preparation and the transfer of the body, the pastor and other ministers are to ensure that the funeral directors appreciate the values and beliefs of the Christian community.

While this booklet allows you to help and guide your survivors in their decisions at the time of your death, it does not intend to exclude family members and friends from the process of preparation for your funeral and burial. Being part of those preparations is an important way that we mourn one another. If you have attended to some details beforehand, your family may then be free to do those simple and beautiful tasks that can be a wholesome part of separation and mourning. Among these could be the washing and clothing of your body. Many funeral directors, if asked, will gladly allow family members to take part in this. Catholics affirm that the body is the temple of the Holy Spirit and insist that the body be treated with a great reverence. This reverence is not expressed in expensive coffins and lavish arrangements but in the very human tasks associated with preparing the body for burial.

☐ I would like my family to take part in the preparation of my body.

☐ I prefer that only the funeral home or crematorium prepare my body.

☐ I prefer that I am not embalmed.

---

4. *Order of Christian Funerals*, 19.
5. As quoted on "The Conversation," an online news source: https://theconversation.com/when-someone-dies-what-happens-to-the-body-143070.

Personal Effects and Keepsakes

There may be certain pieces of jewelry or other accessories that you often wore in life, such as wedding bands, earrings, necklaces, and eyeglasses. The funeral home staff will make sure your wishes are recorded. Keep in mind that these items would need to be removed if you are requesting natural burial (see pages 42–44).

I would like to be buried in this article of clothing:

_____

_____

I would like the following item(s) to be placed in my hand:

_____

_____

I would like the following items to be placed inside my casket/coffin:

_____

_____

Funeral homes will provide families with keepsakes. The Catholic Church does not allow some of these options to take place, such as making jewelry or other items from cremated remains. However, your family members will appreciate the option of having a lock of hair or the imprint of your hand or finger print, either from a digital or clay imprint. Some funeral homes even make a cast of your hand.

I would like the funeral home to provide the following keepsake(s) for my family members: _____

_____

_____

Cremation

Cremation, the practice of burning the body of a deceased person, may be a confusing issue for Catholics. At one time, cremation had not been permitted by the Catholic Church because cremation could be interpreted as an action opposed to the Church's belief in the resurrection of the body on the last day. However, today people do not usually choose cremation as a public statement against Catholic teaching, but rather for a variety of practical reasons. For example, some choose cremation as an affordable alternative to traditional burial. There may be issues involved in transporting the body of an elderly parent who will be buried in a location other than where the person lived at the time of death. Some prefer that their remains not be buried in the ground. Others do not want to be embalmed. If you are uncertain about your own wishes, it would be a wise practice to consult with your pastor or local office of Catholic cemeteries. They will be able to help guide your decisions.

The Church teaches:

> The long-standing practice of burying the body of the deceased in a grave or tomb in imitation of the burial of Jesus' body continues to be encouraged as a sign of Christian faith. However, owing to contemporary cultural interaction, the practice of cremation has become part of Catholic practice in the United States and other parts of the Western world. . . .
>
> Sometimes . . . it is not possible for the body to be present for the funeral liturgy. While promoting the values that underlie our preference for burial of the body, we must exercise sensitive pastoral judgment concerning [this] choice. . . . Economic, geographic, ecological, or family factors on occasion make the cremation of a body the only feasible choice.[6]

It is projected that by 2040 the US cremation rate will reach 78.4 percent.[7] Cremation arrangements are most commonly made either through a funeral home or through membership in a cremation society. As with funeral and cemetery goods and services, you may choose to prepay for your cremation goods and services. Cremation societies often advertise on the obituary pages of local newspapers, and you should contact as many as possible to obtain product and price lists for comparison. People should be aware that there are significant environmental concerns with cremation, such as the releasing of harmful toxins (such as mercury and carbon dioxide) as well as the extended use of fossil fuels.[8]

The Church does prefer that the body be present at the funeral rites. The Church's main concern is that the dignity of the human body and our reverence for it not be compromised in any way. It is the presence of the body at the funeral rites that confronts us with the mystery of life and death—a mystery that should not be glossed over or denied.

> The body which lies in death naturally recalls the personal story of faith, the loving family bonds, the friendships, and the words and acts of kindness of the deceased person. Indeed, the human body is inextricably associated with the human person.[9]

In addition to these "natural" concerns for the human body, there are also supernatural considerations, most notably in the faith life of the deceased: "The body of a deceased Catholic Christian is also the body once washed in Baptism,

---

6. *Reflections on the Body, Cremation, and Catholic Funeral Rites* by the Committee on the Liturgy of the National Conference of Catholic Bishops (now the Committee on Divine Worship of the United States Conference of Catholic Bishops); 1996, 13 and 14.

7. Statistic provided by the National Funeral Director Association 2020 Cremation and Burial Report, published July 2020.

8. If you are concerned about the environmental issues surrounding death, refer to pages 42–44 in this resource.

9. *Order of Christian Funerals*, 411.

anointed with the oil of salvation, and fed with the Bread of Life."[10] The Catholic faith understands the human body as part of the body of Christ and as a temple of the Holy Spirit. Therefore, the body is destined for future glory at the resurrection of the dead.

Nevertheless, the Church understands there are valid reasons why a person might choose to be cremated before the funeral rites take place. The liturgies may be celebrated in the presence of the cremated remains. The same reverence and care given to the body must also be given to the cremated remains.

There are many different options for the timing of cremation. For example, you may arrange for the funeral rites to be celebrated in the presence of the body, with cremation following the funeral Mass. Or you may arrange for direct cremation without embalming before death, before any funeral liturgy. In this case, the cremated remains may be brought to church for the funeral Mass. Not every funeral home or cremation society offers every option, and you may need to contact several cremation service providers to find one that will meet your needs. (Refer to chapter 6 regarding your funeral liturgy plans.)

- ☐ I want to be cremated, but I would like my body to be present at the funeral rites.
- ☐ I want to be cremated immediately; my cremated remains can be present at the Church's funeral rites. I understand that this will affect the way the liturgies are celebrated.

The Coffin or Casket

The coffin or casket is often the single most expensive item in a traditional funeral. In 2021, the average price for a metal coffin was $2,500. On your visits to funeral homes be sure to obtain coffin price lists for comparison. However, coffins themselves may be purchased from sources other than a funeral home, and you might find it productive to research other providers. A simple search online will provide you with many coffin retailers, coffin creators, woodworkers, and retailers (even COSTCO sells coffins!). Some religious communities make their own coffins and caskets that may be purchased by the general public, such as the Trappist monks of New Melleray Abbey, Iowa (https://trappistcaskets.com).

The coffin or casket should be dignified and beautiful. Robert Hovda has written of the coffin in this way:

> The container for the dead body of a believer should be honestly that, and beautiful as simple and well-crafted things are beautiful. The liturgical books of the church tell us that "any kind of pomp or display should be avoided." . . . The dead body as the sign of the person is what demands

---

10. *Order of Christian Funerals*, 412.

honor and reverence, not the coffin. The coffin is the container whose only purpose is to frame and transport the body. There are times in life for festival excess, but this moment is too sacred for that. It is a reflective moment of truth and of farewell, so it wants and demands sturdy, honest, straightforward, basic talk and action and objects. One's death or the death of a loved one is too fundamentally important for make-believe and tinsel, or for simulating the bedroom or the couch.[11]

If you wish to be cremated, there are some additional concerns that you should be aware of. If a coffin is desired, it must be one that is suitable for cremation—generally, one that is made of solid wood or a cloth-covered wood composite. However, a coffin is not required for cremation, and all funeral homes must provide what the federal Funeral Rule calls "alternative containers," heavy cardboard containers intended to be used for cremation. These alternative containers provide a certain economy over coffins when cremation is desired. However, in order to balance economy with a desire to maintain dignity at the celebration of funeral rites where the body is to be present, you may wish to ask the funeral homes about their rental casket, leasing a simple but noble casket for viewing and funeral rites, and purchasing an alternative container for cremation.

☐ I have made the following arrangements for a casket/coffin:

_____
_____
_____

☐ I have not made arrangements for a casket/coffin. These are my wishes:

_____
_____
_____

☐ I wish to be cremated and will need an urn instead of a casket/coffin (see pages 32–34).

The Urn

If you plan to be cremated, an urn will need to be purchased for burial. An urn is a container, sometimes shaped like a vase, which holds the cremated remains of a deceased person. Once the cremated remains have been placed inside, the urn is usually sealed closed.

---

11. "The Amen Corner," *Worship* 59: 258.

The Church emphasizes that "the cremated remains of a body should be treated with the same respect given to the human body from which they come. This includes the use of a worthy vessel to contain the ashes, the manner in which they are carried, the care and attention to appropriate placement and transport, and the final disposition."[12]

You will be able to prepurchase urns from the funeral home. You can also prepurchase urns from your diocesan office of Catholic cemeteries.

☐ I do not wish to be cremated.

☐ I do not want to be cremated and wish to be buried in a coffin/casket (see pages 34–35).

☐ I have made the following arrangements for an urn:

_____
_____
_____

☐ I have not made arrangements for an urn. These are my wishes:

_____
_____
_____

Repatriation of the Body

Many who have immigrated to the United States wish for their bodily remains or cremated remains to be transferred to their home country for funeral services and burial. It can be complicated for families to contact the local embassy or consulate and so it is best to work with a local funeral home. They will be able to secure the proper paperwork needed to transport the body and work out details with a funeral home and church in the home country. This paperwork includes the following:

- death certificate with the cause of death
- permit for the international transit of the body or ashes issued by the state health authority
- embalming certificate (not necessary in case of cremation)
- certificate of noncontagious diseases (not necessary in case of cremation)
- cremation certificate (only in the case of cremation)

---

12. *Order of Christian Funerals*, 417.

Because of COVID-19, stricter guidelines have been put in place for bodily transport. For example, Mexico requires more detailed embalming, and the body must be sealed in a bio-sealed bag within the sealed coffin or casket. The embassy or consulate may grant permission for the family to transport cremated remains themselves. If a person has died for COVID-19, there is a chance the body won't be allowed into the country unless it has been cremated.

☐ I wish to be buried in my home country (note country here):
_____

☐ I have explored the state and international rules concerning transport of my body.

☐ Family members should contact this local funeral home to prepare for the transport of my body.

Funeral home: _____

Contact person: _____

Address: _____

_____

Telephone: _____

Email/website: _____

Here are my special requests for the funeral home and church in my home country: _____

_____

_____

_____

The transport of the body doesn't just affect those seeking burial in other countries. Sometimes, a person might be living in one state and wish to be buried in another state, most likely a state in which other family members are buried. In this case, a funeral home in the place where you are living at the time of death should be contacted in order to procure the proper paperwork for transport. You may wish to contact a local funeral home ahead of time to negotiate these arrangements. You will also need to contact a local parish church should liturgies be celebrated locally and the parish church who will handle your burial (especially if additional liturgies will be celebrated in the state of your choosing).

☐ I wish to be buried in another state (note state here):
_____

☐ I have made arrangements with the following funeral home for transport.

Funeral home: _____

Contact person: _____

Address: _____

_____

Telephone: _____

Email/website: _____

Add additional information here concerning funeral services and burial in another state:

_____

_____

_____

If you have additional requests regarding the funeral home, caskets, urns, etc., please add them here: _____

_____

_____

_____

_____

_____

_____

_____

_____

_____

_____

_____

CHAPTER FOUR

Cemetery Arrangements

> In committing the body to its resting place, the community expresses the hope that, with all those who have gone before marked with the sign of faith, the deceased awaits the glory of the resurrection.
> —*Order of Christian Funerals*, 206

Burial

It is an act of mercy to bury the dead, and is an action that respects the inherent, God-given dignity of a person's body or cremated remains.[1] Purchasing a burial plot is not a real estate transaction; it is securing your right to be interred, which is an act of Catholic faith.

> Following the most ancient Christian tradition, the Church insistently recommends that the bodies of the deceased be buried in cemeteries or other sacred places. In memory of the death, burial and resurrection of the Lord, the mystery that illumines the Christian meaning of death, burial is above all the most fitting way to express faith and hope in the resurrection of the body. The Church who, as Mother, has accompanied the Christian during his earthly pilgrimage, offers to the Father, in Christ, the child of her grace, and she commits to the earth, in hope, the seed of the body that will rise in glory. By burying the bodies of the faithful, the Church confirms her faith in the resurrection of the body, and intends to show the great dignity of the human body as an integral part of the human person whose body forms part of their identity.[2]

---

1. In the Catholic tradition, cremated remains are to be interred or buried.
2. Instruction of Pope Francis, *Ad resurgendum cum Christo* (*Regarding the Burial of the Deceased and the Conservation of Ashes in the Cases of Cremation*), 3. This document may be accessed on the Vatican website (www.vatican.va).

Although Catholics may be buried in public cemeteries or places of internment, consider choosing a Catholic cemetery. Catholic cemeteries are often available for the entire diocese, or individual parishes might have their own. When possible, choosing a Catholic cemetery has many advantages. Not only is the entire cemetery sacred ground and a place for the regular gathering of prayer, its sole mission guarantees that every burial professes our belief in the communion of the saints and, above all, stands as a vivid witness to the resurrection of the dead. If you are uncertain if there is a Catholic cemetery near you, contact your pastor or diocesan office of Catholic cemeteries.

Larger cemeteries offer many options for location, family plots, memorial markers, above-ground entombment in mausoleums, and placement of cremated remains. Some of the costs associated with the cemetery can include the price of the lot, burial vault or grave liner (if required by the cemetery), vault or liner installation charge, opening and closing charges (typically higher on weekends), marker installation charge, and the cemetery "counselor's" commission. Not every cemetery offers the same prepurchasing options. Some can sell plots but do not have permits for sale of items or services to be delivered in the future. Burial plots can range dramatically in price; however, the average cost for full body burial ranges from $525 to $5,000; burial for cremated remains can range from $350 to $2500.[3]

Markers themselves may be purchased from sources other than the cemetery. Local newspaper obituary pages (and even parish bulletins) often have advertisements from companies that provide markers for retail sale, or search online for local companies. Many cemeteries require either a burial vault or a grave liner into which the coffin is placed. The vault or liner is typically made of reinforced concrete and is meant to prevent the ground from shifting. You will need to explore what is or isn't allowed to take place at the cemetery you have chosen. The following website provides a basic overview regarding US law and cemeteries: https://www.stimmel-law.com/en/articles/basic-laws-pertaining-cemeteries. The following website also provides information regarding individual states and their burial laws: https://www.wcl.american.edu/burial/.

As with funeral home goods and services, you may choose to prepay for your cemetery goods and services. Again, be sure you are making an informed decision. Gather price lists from two or three cemeteries. Use the information you gather to prepare a brief statement about what you consider important features of your burial.

Many cemeteries have on-site funeral homes that are either owned by the cemetery or are contracted by the cemetery to operate on cemetery property. Do not assume that the combination funeral home and cemetery will automatically be the best choice for all your needs. Veterans should be aware that they,

---

3. This 2021 statistic is provided by Consumer Resources; available at https://www.lhlic.com/consumer-resources/burial-plot-cost/.

their spouses, and their dependent children are entitled to burial without cost in a national cemetery.[4]

Catholics should be aware that "cremated remains should be buried in a grave or entombed in a mausoleum or columbarium. The practice of scattering cremated remains on the sea, from the air, or on the ground, or keeping cremated remains in the home of a relative or friend of the deceased are not the reverent disposition that the Church requires."[5] This includes burying cremated remains in biodegradable vessels or fashioning the cremated remains into jewelry, paper weights, or other keepsakes. Cremated remains should also not be divided among family members.

While there are several options for the disposition of the body and cremated remains, the Christian community always marks the moment with prayer. The Church's funeral rite provides that the place of committal be blessed as a place of honor in expectation of the glory of the resurrection. (Refer to chapter 6.)

☐ I have decided to prepay for my burial arrangements.

Name of cemetery: _____

Contact person: _____

Address: _____

_____

Telephone: _____

Email/website: _____

Name of lot or crypt holder: _____

Easement or deed number: _____

Legal description of graves or crypt as shown on easement or deed can be noted here: _____

_____

_____

_____

Other burial goods or services can be noted here: _____

_____

_____

_____

The contract is kept: _____

_____

---

4. In this context, burial is literal—it does not include coffins, transfer to the cemetery, or services.
5. *Order of Christian Funerals*, 417.

☐ I am a lot holder and have made arrangement with the cemetery to assign graves to specific individuals. The arrangements are:

_____
_____
_____

Grave number: _____

Assigned to: _____

☐ I have decided not to prepay for burial goods and services. I suggest the following arrangements for plot, crypt, etc.:

_____
_____
_____
_____

☐ I would like to be buried in a Catholic cemetery.

Natural Burial

As people become more and more concerned with climate change and respecting the environment, it is natural that questions will arise about the preparation of the body and burial. Cremation emits harmful toxins and uses fossil fuels, and the embalming of the body uses harmful chemicals such as formaldehyde. You might be exploring more eco-friendly options for your own funeral arrangements.

> Green burials allow returning to the earth in a manner that interacts with, rather than impedes, the natural process of decay and regeneration. A family forgoes embalming their loved one's body with toxic chemicals and avoids non-biodegradable metal caskets and burial vaults. Instead, the deceased, often washed by family members, is wrapped in a shroud or placed in a simple wooden casket before being lowered into the ground. Some families even choose to help dig the grave rather than to rely on heavy, energy-intensive equipment.[6]

> Green burials invite us to get up close and personal with our end-of-life rituals. Rather than handing over responsibilities to others, families can get involved with everything from body preparation to grave decorating to almost anything else they deem important for honoring the dead, healing the living, and inviting in the divine. It also doesn't take away options many families have found comfort in, such

---

6. From Joe Sehee, published in *U.S. Catholic*, "Think outside the Box: Being Green at the End of Life," *U.S. Catholic* (October 6, 2011): https://uscatholic.org/articles/201110/think-outside-the-box-being-green-at-the-end-of-life/; accessed November 1, 2016.

as public visitations, open-casket funerals, and even cremation. The end result is often a great deal of solace.

You might wonder what options for an eco-friendly funeral you have as a Catholic. Catholics are to be buried in sacred, or blessed, ground, and the dignity of the body is the guiding principle for preparing and burying the body. "The body . . . brings to mind that our human bodies are temples of the Holy Spirit, destined for future glory . . . the body that lies in death recalls the personal story of faith, the past relationships, and the continued spiritual presence of the deceased person."[7] More and more Catholic cemeteries are taking heed of Pope Francis' concern for the environment and are becoming more adept at natural burials that respect the earth.

> The term natural burial represents a broader spectrum of burial options than does green burial which is more definite and conservation-based. An existing cemetery that adds a natural burial section determines the rules, regulations, and limitations while maintaining the integrity that is foundational to the values of green burial. . . .
>
> In the natural-burial process, the body of the deceased, and the earth to which the body returns, are treated with reverence. The body is not embalmed with chemicals nor is it enclosed in a typical casket and lowered into a concrete vault. Instead, during the natural-burial process, the body of the deceased may be wrapped in a natural-fiber shroud or placed in a container made of biodegradable material such as unfinished wood or wicker, and buried at a site that is dedicated to natural burial.[8]

Although state laws vary, with a green or natural burial the body would need to be buried quickly. The average time after death before embalming becomes necessary is 48 to 72 hours. You should also be aware that some state laws prevent the viewing of a body that is not embalmed, or restrict the viewing to immediate family only. The option for a natural burial would also need to be provided by the cemetery itself.

If you are concerned about environmentally friendly or natural burials, be sure to discuss these needs with the funeral home of your choice and the cemetery in which you would like to be buried. You might contact your pastor or diocesan office of Catholic cemeteries for additional information about local options. More information may be found on the website of the Green Burial Council: https://www.greenburialcouncil.org/the-catholic-church-and-green-burial.html.

☐ I would like an environmentally friendly burial.

---

7. *Reflections on the Body, Cremation, and Catholic Funeral Rites*, 13; referencing 1 Corinthians 6:19.
8. From the website of The Catholic Cemeteries which resides in the Archdiocese of Minneapolis St. Paul (www.catholic-cemeteries.org). This organization is certified by the Green Burial Council. This website provides additional information about Catholics and environmentally friendly burials. Used with permission.

☐ I have researched this type of burial and would like the following arrangements (include funeral home, cemetery, and parish information):

_____
_____
_____

Private Burial

Some people choose to bury their own dead. People who take this option should know the local legislation that governs the disposal of bodies, and they must be able to carry out the tasks of private burial. This might include hosting the wake or vigil service in one's home (see chapter 6). The following website provides burial laws organized by state: https://coeio.com/burial-laws-state/. And this website provides state-specific information for private burials on your home property: https://www.romemonuments.com/home-burials. If you wish to be buried in a private military cemetery, you will need to contact the US Department of Veterans Affairs: https://www.va.gov/burials-memorials/eligibility/burial-in-private-cemetery/.

☐ I wish to have a private burial. Here are my arrangments:

_____
_____
_____

Memorial Marker and Inscription

Whether the body is committed to a grave, tomb, mausoleum, or columbarium, the place of committal should have a memorial marker. The placing of a gravestone is usually a labor-intensive procedure, planned according to the schedule of the fabricator, the cemetery, and the weather. Families may wish to regather soon after the stone has been placed. The Church even provides a blessing for the burial marker. Gravestones and markers are made in a variety of materials and sizes; some are upright, and others lay flat. Still some are more grandiose in design and might include common holy figures such as Mary and angels. Typically the markers include one's name, birth date, and death date. Some might choose to inscribe a short phrase or quotation, or even a photograph of the deceased. You may purchase markers from your local office of Catholic cemeteries or from a private company. Be sure you are aware of which markers are allowed at your burial plot.

☐ I have arrangements for a memorial marker with the following company or organization.

Name: _____

Contact person: _____

Address: _____

_____

Telephone: _____

Email/website: _____

☐ I have not made arrangements for a memorial marker.

I would like the following information on my memorial marker (include quotations, symbols, etc.): _____

_____

_____

Inscribe my name and birth/death dates as:

_____

Grave Decorations

The families of loved ones should know that cemeteries will have rules regarding decorations. They should be aware of what is allowed where you will be interred. In general, fresh or artificial flowers, wreaths, monument vases, and small flags are allowed. Cemeteries might restrict the use of fencing, vessels made of glass, stakes in the ground, stuffed animals, or other free-standing objects. Check to see what your cemetery allows so that there will be little conflict with family members in the future.

My additional burial concerns and requests:

_____
_____
_____
_____
_____
_____
_____
_____
_____
_____

CHAPTER FIVE

Obituary and Memorial Information

In your kindness remember me . . .
—Psalm 25:7b

Obituary

Obituaries and death notices include information about one's life and family. The funeral home or cremation society will post the obituary on their website as part of their services. Obituaries may of course be printed in the newspaper; the funeral home will often help families with this task. The average cost for printing an obituary in the newspaper can range from one hundred to eight hundred dollars. The newspapers will also post the obituaries on their websites and link the post to the funeral home website. Grieving friends and family members will be able to leave comments, share pictures, and add candle icons in an act of prayer. Some family members might choose to create a memorial website or turn the deceased person's Facebook page into a memorial page (see below). Obituaries are a wonderful way for family and friends to remember you and they provide genealogists with written records of life. By filling out the following pages carefully and completely, you will leave these needed records. You can also find free obituary templates online, such as: https://www.obituaryguide.com/template.php.

Biographical Information

Full name: _____

Name before marriage: _____

Date of birth: _____

Place of birth: _____
_____

Baptism (church, location, date): _____
_____

Married to: _____

Place and date of marriage: _____
_____

Previous marriages: _____

Parents' names: _____

Parent's place of residence: _____
_____

Parent's date of birth and death: _____
_____

Name of children (including married name): _____
_____
_____
_____

Children's residence: _____
_____
_____

Children's date of birth and death: _____
_____
_____

Names of grandchildren and great-grandchildren: _____
_____
_____
_____

Names of brothers and sisters, other relatives:
_____
_____

Obituary and Memorial Information

Education

    School: _____

    Location: _____

    Dates: _____

    Diploma/degree: _____

Military Service

    Branch of service: _____

    Serial number: _____

    Dates of service and rank: _____

    Veterans Affairs claim number: _____

    Death benefits: _____

    Location of discharge papers: _____

Work History

    Position: _____

    Location: _____

    Dates: _____

    Union membership: _____

Previous residences

    City/State: _____

    Dates: _____

    Accomplishments and honors: _____

    _____

    _____

    Hobbies/interests: _____

    _____

    _____

Additional things to note in your obituary may be added here: _____

_____
_____
_____
_____
_____

Prayer or Memorial Cards

In many places it is customary to have prayer or memorial cards that list the name, dates of birth and death, and sometimes other information about the deceased. These cards often have religious images and texts from Scripture or prayers. Funeral homes may offer a selection of such cards with an image and prayer already printed on them, but the family may choose to have a simple card prepared and printed before the wake and funeral. You may wish to specify a particular image, Scripture text, or prayer for your memorial card.

☐ I would like the following to be on my prayer or memorial card.

Image: _____

Scripture verse: _____

_____
_____

Prayer: _____

_____
_____

Is there anything else you might wish to include on the card? _____

_____
_____
_____

Memorial Requests

Flowers and contributions to charities are customary memorials given by family and friends at the time of death. Many people prefer to give specific memorials in accordance with the wishes of the deceased. These wishes are usually printed in the obituary and death notices. Indicate any special preference for memorials. Sometimes parish churches have rules regarding the placement of flowers. The pastor or bereavement minister will be able to help your family. In some cases, flowers are best left at the funeral home and then transferred to the place of committal. Following the funeral liturgies, family and friends may take the flowers home.

☐ I would prefer memorial donations be made to the following organization(s) instead of flowers:

_____
_____

☐ I am comfortable with my family making memorial decisions, flowers, or other options.

Memorial Video

When preparing for the visitation, wake, or viewing, funeral home staff may offer the option of submitting photos and music so that they can create a video that continuously plays during this time (except during prayer services). This is a nice option to fondly remember the deceased and share stories about when photos were taken and recall other family members who have passed on. Sometimes these videos are posted on the funeral home website or social media page and friends and family members are able to comment on the post. A copy of the video may be given to family members following the funeral.

My printed photos are kept:_____
_____

My digital photos are kept: _____
_____

Login:_____

Password:_____

☐ I would like the following pieces of music to be played during the video or visitation:

_____
_____
_____

Memorial Items

Often, family members like to display photographs and items associated with their loved ones at the funeral home or in the vestibule of the church. Perhaps you played guitar, were a quilter or artist, or received medals in the armed forces. Consider what you might like to be displayed.

☐ I would like photographs to be displayed (see above for information).

☐ I would like the following items to be displayed:

_____

_____

_____

☐ I don't have special requests and trust that family members will honor me in their own way.

Social Media

Social media (or YouTube) may even be used to broadcast the funeral liturgies. Livestreaming the liturgies enables family members unable to attend the funeral to take part in their own way. You will need to make live streaming arrangements with the funeral home director and the pastor of the church where the funeral will take place.

☐ I would like my funeral liturgies to be livestreamed.

☐ I would not like my funeral liturgies to be livestreamed.

Memorial Luncheon or Dinner

Family and friends may gather for a meal after the liturgy or burial. This may take place in a person's home, at a restaurant, or at the parish hall. You should consult your parish church if this is an option for families.

Here are my wishes for a funeral luncheon or dinner:

_____

_____

_____

Here are additional requests that I have concerning obituary and memorials:

_____

_____

_____

CHAPTER SIX

Catholic Funeral Services or Rites

> Christians celebrate the funeral rites to offer worship, praise, and thanksgiving to God for the gift of a life which has now been returned to God, the author of life and the hope of the just.
> —*Order of Christian Funerals*, 5

In the time following a death, the Christian community surrounds the bereaved with support and prayer as they recall the life of the departed, express their sorrow, renew their faith in Christ, and bid farewell in the hope of the resurrection. The celebration of the funeral rites offers the family and other mourners a path through the initial period of grief to the committal of their loved one's earthly remains to their place of rest. The Church accompanies them on this path, expressing God's love for those who have died and for those who mourn.

The three primary Catholic funeral rites, the Vigil for the Deceased, the Funeral Liturgy, and the Rite of Committal, are stops along this path. Each of these rites consists of familiar elements of Catholic liturgy: Scripture readings, responsorial psalms, and music. (Refer to pages 62–65 for Scripture suggestions and pages 65–66 for music suggestions.)

These rituals affirm and express solidarity between the living and the dead in the communion of saints. When preparing your own funeral rites, approach these rituals as one prayer, like a procession that moves from the deathbed to the place of committal.

☐ Please contact the following parish upon news of my death to make arrangements for my funeral services.

Name of Church:_____

Contact person:_____

Address: _____

_____

Telephone: _____

Email/website: _____

The Vigil for the Deceased

The Vigil for the Deceased, sometimes referred to as the wake service, takes place during the wake, visitation, or viewing—the first gathering of extended family and friends after the death. This service brings to prayer the pain and sorrow of those present and gives voice to the comforting presence of God. The Vigil respectfully acknowledges the earthly life of the deceased and all the relationships that sustained them in this world.

The Vigil for the Deceased most often takes place at a funeral home, although some parishes are able to accommodate the visitation in the church or another suitable space. It may also take place in the family home. The Vigil service usually takes place at the end of the time for visitation. When preparing the details for your visitation, consider where you would like this to take place.

The Vigil for the Deceased is the official rite of the Church and is different than praying the Rosary or other prayers at the time of the visitation, viewing, or wake. The Vigil is usually celebrated as a Liturgy of the Word, much like the first half of Mass. A priest, deacon, or layperson may lead the service. Customarily, the parish provides the leader.

Usually during the wake, there is time for guests to offer their condolences to surviving family members and share stories, as well as offer final respects to the person who has died. At a designated time, and when all guests are seated, the Vigil service begins. Members of the family or funeral home staff may assist with inviting those who may be conversing to take a seat and observe a moment of silence. It is helpful to provide a worship aid for those who participate, particularly for those who may not be Catholic. Your parish staff will be able to help family members prepare a simple worship aid.

The leader of the service may invite those assembled to stand, if appropriate, and then greet them. They respond as they would at Mass. An opening song is then sung. This song should be familiar to as many people in attendance as possible and simple to sing. A traditional hymn or repetitive chant may serve well. Ideally, an instrumentalist and a song leader is present to lead the singing, but this is often not the case. The prayer leader or other person might be asked to start the singing. After the song, the leader offers a prayer, to which all respond, "Amen." All are then seated.

Two Scripture readings with a responsorial psalm between them are proclaimed. The first reading is from either the Old Testament or, if the funeral takes place during the Easter season, a New Testament letter. A person other than the leader may proclaim it. The responsorial psalm follows and, ideally, it is sung. Most parish musicians will have settings of these psalms. Otherwise, the psalm is spoken. The second reading is taken from a Gospel. It is usually proclaimed by the one who is leading the Vigil, who then offers a brief homily or reflection on the readings. (Refer to pages 62–65 for Scripture suggestions and pages 65–66 for music suggestions.)

A litany of intercession, which may be led by someone other than the leader, is prayed. The Lord's Prayer and a concluding prayer follow. At this point, a friend or family member may speak in remembrance of the deceased person.

A blessing follows, which includes this traditional prayer. If a worship aid is prepared, this prayer should be part of it.

> Eternal rest grant unto him/her/them, O Lord,
>   and let perpetual light shine upon him/her/them.
> May he/she/they rest in peace. Amen.
> May his/her/their soul(s) and all the souls of the faithful
>   departed, through the mercy of God, rest in peace. Amen.[1]

A moment of silence or a song may conclude the Vigil.

If the visitation takes place in the church where the funeral liturgy is to be celebrated, the body may be received into the church as is usually done at the beginning of the Funeral Liturgy, with the placing of the pall, the placing of a Christian symbol upon the casket or coffin, and the sprinkling with holy water (or even incensation). The Vigil for the Deceased follows, with the visitation afterward. In that case, reception of the body is not to be repeated at the Funeral Liturgy.

If the Vigil for the Deceased takes place in a home, the service may be simplified. The parish pastor will be able to assist with this.

While the Vigil for the Deceased usually occurs in the context of a Liturgy of the Word, it may be celebrated in the context of Morning or Evening Prayer. This is more likely to be done in a community that regularly celebrates the hours, such as a religious community. If you often pray the Liturgy of the Hours and would like this to be done as your Vigil service, the parish community will be able to help your family prepare this service.

I would like the vigil service to take place:

☐ In my home.

☐ At the parish church.

☐ At the funeral home.

☐ I have no requests.

---

1. *Order of Christian Funerals*, 81.

☐ I would like the Liturgy of the Hours to be prayed as my Vigil service.

I would like the following person(s) to offer words of remembrance at the Vigil service: _____

Although my parish community will probably designate a minister to officiate the Vigil service, I would like that the following person to lead:
_____

☐ It doesn't matter to me who leads the service.

I would like the following persons to read the Scripture and Litany:
_____
_____

I would like the following person(s) to lead the music:
_____
_____

The Vigil for the Deceased: Outline of Service

Scripture may be chosen from the options provided on pages 62–65. Music may be chosen from the options provided on pages 65–66.

Introductory Rite
- Greeting
- Sprinkling with Holy Water
- [Placing of the Pall]
- Entrance Procession/ Opening Song
- [Placing of Christian Symbols]
- Invitation to Prayer
- Opening Prayer

Liturgy of the Word
- First Reading
  (Old or New Testament)
- Responsorial Psalm
- Gospel
- Homily/Reflection

Prayer of Intercession
- Litany
- The Lord's Prayer
- Concluding Prayer
- Words of Remembrance

Concluding Rite
- Blessing
- [Closing Song]

I would like the following music sung at my Vigil
(see pages 65–66 for options): _____
_____
_____
_____

I would like the following Scripture readings proclaimed at my Vigil

(see pages 62–65 for options): _____
_____
_____
_____

The Funeral Liturgy

The Funeral Liturgy is the main Catholic liturgical celebration for dead. It reflects on the life and death of this one Christian in the context of the Paschal Mystery of Jesus Christ—his life, death, and resurrection—through whom we have been redeemed and given the promise of eternal life. The Funeral Liturgy also calls to mind others who have died in Christ, renewing our hope that they also rest in the peace of Christ. It may also remind us of our own mortality, of God's presence in our own life, and of our own hope for eternal life.

The Funeral Liturgy is preferably and most commonly a celebration of the Eucharist, although it may be a Liturgy of the Word with the Final Commendation.

Introductory Rites

This promise of eternal life was given to us at our baptism. The Funeral Liturgy explicitly recalls this event. The remains of the deceased, and their accompanying loved ones, are greeted at the door of the church by the celebrant. The celebrant is accompanied by a minister who carries a processional cross as a reminder that on the day of baptism, the deceased was claimed for Christ by the sign of the cross.

The celebrant sprinkles the casket or urn with holy water, a reminder that this person died and rose with Christ in baptism. A large cloth, a pall, may be placed on the casket as a reminder of their baptismal garment, a sign of their Christian dignity. Another Christian symbol, such as a crucifix or a Bible, may also be placed on the casket. Clothed in the signs of their baptism, the deceased is brought in procession to lie in repose before the altar, usually accompanied by a hymn. If cremated remains are present instead of your body, the remains are not draped in an alb and a symbol is not used. Your family may carry your urn to where it will be placed during the Funeral Liturgy. (Refer to pages 65–66 for music suggestions.)

The Paschal candle, which was first lit on the night of the Easter Vigil as a symbol of the Christ our light, stands nearby. When the hymn has ended and everyone is at their seats, the celebrant concludes the introductory rites with the Collect, or opening prayer.

Liturgy of the Word

During the Liturgy of the Word it is preferable that two Scripture readings precede the Gospel reading, although there may be just one. If there are two readings, one is taken from the Old Testament and one from the New Testament. If there is only one non-Gospel reading, it may be taken from either the Old or the New Testament. During Easter Time, the first reading may be taken from the Acts of the Apostles. The non-Gospel readings are proclaimed by a lay reader, preferably one for each reading, with experience in proclamation. A responsorial psalm, preferably sung, follows the first reading. The celebrant proclaims the Gospel and offers a brief homily. (Refer to pages 62–65 for Scripture suggestions.)

After the conclusion of the homily, the celebrant introduces the universal prayer or prayer of the faithful. The intercessions are read by another minister, and all respond. The parish church may provide intercessions, but new ones may be composed that include the intentions of the family of the deceased.

Liturgy of the Eucharist

If the funeral is taking place without Mass, the Liturgy of the Eucharist is omitted and the liturgy continues with the Final Commendation.

At a Funeral Mass, the Liturgy of the Eucharist is celebrated in the usual manner. Friends or family members may be invited to present the gifts of bread and wine for the Mass to the celebrant. A song or instrumental music accompanies the procession and preparation of the gifts. The acclamations of the Eucharistic Prayer—the Sanctus, the memorial acclamation and the Amen are sung. A Communion song is sung throughout the reception of Communion by the assembly. A song or hymn appropriate to the celebration may be sung after Communion.

Final Commendation

Before the final commendation begins, a friend or family member may speak briefly in remembrance of the deceased person if diocesan and parish guidelines permit.

Before the mourners depart from the church, they bid farewell to the deceased, calling upon the saints and angels to accompany the soul of the dead into the presence of God and beseeching God to bestow rest and peace upon them. During this time, the celebrant may honor the body with incense, in recognition that it is a temple of the Holy Spirit. A final prayer commending the soul of the departed to the God of mercy and an invitation to accompany the dead to the place of rest conclude the service. For many attending the funeral, this may be the last moment in the presence of the deceased. For those who will accompany the body to the cemetery, it is a preparation for the final moment of farewell.

If the body of the deceased was received into the church with the sprinkling of water before the Vigil, it is not received in that manner again. In that case, the Funeral Liturgy begins with a procession to the altar accompanied by a hymn, as at Sunday Mass.

Even if the pall and other Christian symbols are not placed on the casket, no other symbols or objects may be placed on it during the liturgy. This includes national flags, insignia of civic or religious organizations, and symbols of the person's trade or hobbies.

The decision may be made to celebrate the Funeral Liturgy outside Mass for a good reason. Such reasons include the need to hold the funeral on a day when a funeral Mass is not permitted by the Church (such as Good Friday), the lack of an available priest before the burial is to take place, or the family and pastor may decide together that it is more suitable for pastoral reasons. The Funeral Liturgy outside Mass is usually celebrated in a parish church, but may also celebrated in other settings, such as a funeral home or cemetery chapel. A priest, deacon, or layperson may lead the service.

When the choice has been made to cremate a body, the Church prefers that the body of the deceased be present for the various funeral rites, and that cremation follow the funeral Mass. However, when cremation takes place shortly after death, it is appropriate that the cremated remains of the body be present during the vigil service and the funeral liturgy. However, certain rites cannot take place with the cremated remains, such as the placing of the pall and the sprinkling of holy water. These rites are reserved for the body, which was dignified and signed with God's grace at baptism.

I would like the following priest to preside over my funeral: _____
_____

I would like the following persons to read the Scripture and intercessions at my funeral liturgy: _____
_____
_____

I would like the following persons to be involved with the music at my funeral liturgy: _____
_____
_____

☐ I would like my body present at the funeral liturgy. I realize this affects the timing and finances surrounding embalming and cremation.

I would like the following persons (men and women may be chosen) to be involved as pall bearers, to place the Christian symbol on my coffin, or to bring up the gifts of bread and wine:_____

_____

_____

I would like the following persons to serve as hospitality ministers, altar servers, and extraordinary ministers of holy Communion:

_____

_____

I would like the following religious symbol placed on my coffin:_____

_____

I would like the following person to offer words of remembrance:

_____

During the universal prayer at Mass, we pray for the needs of the Church, the world, the oppressed, and the local community. The following needs are important to me and I would like to have them incorporated into this prayer at my funeral:_____

_____

_____

_____

The Funeral Liturgy: Outlines of Services

Music may be chosen from the options provided on pages 65–66. Scripture may be chosen from the options provided on pages 62–65. Select which option you prefer (within Mass or without Mass) from the outlines provided below.

☐ **Option 1: Within Mass**

Introductory Rites
- Greeting
- Sprinkling with Holy Water
- [Placing of the Pall]
- Entrance Procession/ Opening Song
- [Placing of Christian Symbols]
- Collect

☐ **Option 2: Without Mass**

Introductory Rites
- Greeting
- Sprinkling with Holy Water
- [Placing of the Pall]
- Entrance Procession/ Opening Song
- [Placing of Christian Symbols]
- Invitation to Prayer
- Opening Prayer

Catholic Funeral Services or Rites

Continued from previous page

Liturgy of the Word
- First Reading (*Old Testament; New Testament during Easter*)
- Responsorial Psalm
- Second Reading (*New Testament*)
- Gospel Acclamation
- Gospel
- Homily
- Universal Prayer

Liturgy of the Eucharist
- Preparation of the Gifts
- Preface
- Preface Acclamation (*Holy, Holy, Holy*)
- Memorial Acclamation
- Amen

Communion Rite
- Sign of Peace
- Lamb of God
- Communion Song

Final Commendation
- Invitation to Prayer
- Silence
- Signs of Farewell
- Song of Farewell
- Prayer of Commendation
- Closing Song
- Procession to the Place of Committal

Continued from previous page

Liturgy of the Word
- First Reading (*Old Testament; New Testament during Easter*)
- Responsorial Psalm
- Second Reading (*New Testament*)
- Gospel Acclamation
- Gospel
- Homily/Reflection
- Universal Prayer
- The Lord's Prayer

Final Commendation
- Invitation to Prayer
- Silence
- [Signs of Farewell]
- Song of Farewell
- Prayer of Commendation
- Closing Song
- Procession to the Place of Committal

I would like the following music sung at my Funeral Liturgy (see pages 65–66 for options): _____

_____

_____

_____

I would like the following Scripture readings proclaimed at my Funeral Liturgy I (see pages 62–65 for options): _____

_____

_____

_____

_____

The Rite of Committal

The Rite of Committal is the final action of the Church and loved ones for the body of the dead, seeing it safely to the place where it will await the resurrection of the dead and praying together one last time before continuing their own lives in the absence of their loved one. This resting place also becomes a place for prayer and remembrance in the days, months, and years to come.

The rite itself is very brief. After the mourners and ministers arrive at the place of committal, the leader invites all to pray. A brief Scripture passage is read, which focuses on our hope of heaven for the deceased and for all present. Usually the person leading the service will select the short Scripture passage.

After a prayer over the place of committal, the leader speaks words of committal of the body of the deceased to the earth and commendation of their soul to God.

A litany of intercession and the Lord's Prayer follow. The rite concludes with a prayer over the people, the prayer for eternal rest and perpetual life for the deceased, and a dismissal. The rite suggests that a sign of leave-taking may be made by the mourners.

This rite is meant to take place at the actual burial site, such as at the open grave or tomb, rather than at a cemetery chapel. Cemetery regulations, weather, and other realities will affect the final decision of where it takes place. The rite may also take place at the crematorium where the cremation will take place or at a burial at sea.

If no Funeral Liturgy has been celebrated, the Song of Farewell and the Rite of Commendation may be added to the Rite of Committal.

Signs of leave-taking might include walking past the casket and offering a touch or a kiss, or placing a flower on the casket or in the open grave or tomb. If the casket or urn has been lowered into the grave, family members may drop flowers or shovels-full of dirt into the grave.

THE RITE OF COMMITTAL: OUTLINE OF SERVICE

Music may be chosen from the options provided on pages 65–66.

[Opening Song]
Invitation
Scripture Verse (the minister will select a verse)
Prayer over the Place of Committal
Invitation to Payer
Silence
[Signs of Farewell]
[Song of Farewell]
[Prayer of Commendation]
Committal
Prayer over the People
[Closing Song]
Sign of Leave Taking

I would like this minister to preside over my burial: _____
_____

I would like the following music sung at my burial (see pages 65–66 for options):

_____
_____
_____

Scripture Readings

The Church provides many suggestions for Scripture readings. The Old Testament readings proposed proclaim the care of God for his people, but each may seem more appropriate in a particular circumstance, such as when a person has died peacefully in old age or when someone had suffered in their life. The many New Testament selections from the epistles offer various aspects of the understanding of Christian death. Some focus on the death and resurrection of Jesus Christ; others look forward to our own deaths, judgments before God, and resurrections with faith and hope. The readings from the Book of Revelation offer a vision of a new heaven and a new earth. The selections from the Gospels offer excerpts from the teachings of Jesus about those who will be received by God into the heavenly kingdom.

The following readings may be selected for a funeral liturgy with or without Mass. The structure of the Liturgy of the Word at a funeral follows the same order as at Sunday Mass. You will need to select two readings, a responsorial psalm, and a Gospel reading. The readings may also be used at the Vigil (or wake) service. For additional guidance in selecting readings, use *Eternal Rest in the Lord: Preparing the Liturgy of the Word at Catholic Funerals* (Liturgy Training Publications).

Reading 1 from the Old Testament

Select one reading for your Vigil and one reading for the first reading at your Funeral Liturgy.

Maccabees 12:43–46
He acted in an excellent and noble way as he had the resurrection of the dead in view.

Job 19:1, 23–27a
I know that my vindicator lives.

Job 3:1–9 or 3, 1–6, 9
As sacrificial offerings he took them to himself.

Wisdom 4:7–15
An unsullied life, the attainment of old age.

Isaiah 25:6a, 7–9
He will destroy death forever.

Lamentations 3:17–26
It is good to hope in silence for the saving help of the Lord.

Daniel 12:1–3
Many of those who sleep in the dust of the earth shall awake.

Reading 1 from the New Testament during Easter Time

In case your funeral takes place during Easter Time, select one reading for your Vigil and one reading for the first reading at your Funeral Liturgy.

Acts of the Apostles 10:34–43 or 10:34–36, 42–43
He is the one appointed by God as judge of the living and the dead.

Revelation 14:3
Blessed are the dead who die in the Lord.

Revelation 20:11—21:1
The dead were judged according to their deeds.

Revelation 21:1–5a, 6b–7
There shall be no more death.

Responsorial Psalm

All psalms end with trust and hope in God, but some reflect times of hardship and struggle, times when God has protected us, and times when we have longed to know God. Like all the other Scripture options, some may better reflect the one whose life and death we celebrate and mourn. In their origin, psalms are lyrical hymns meant to be sung. Select one psalm for your Vigil service and one psalm for your funeral liturgy. Your parish music director will be able to help with musical options.

Psalm 23:1–3, 4, 5, 7
The Lord is my shepherd.

Psalm 25:6 and 7b, 17–18, 20–21
To you, O Lord, I lift my soul.

Psalm 27:1, 4, 7 and 8b and 9a, 13–14
The Lord is my light and my salvation.

Psalm 42:2, 3, 5cdef; 43:3, 4, 5
My soul is thirsting for the living God.

Psalm 63:2, 3–4, 5–6, 8–9
My soul is thirsting for you, O Lord my God.

Psalm 103:8 and 10, 13–14, 15–16, 17–18
The Lord is kind and merciful.

Psalm 116:5, 6, 10–11, 15–16ac
I will walk in the presence of the Lord in the land of the living.

Psalm 122:1–2, 4–5, 6–7, 8–9
Let us go rejoicing to the house of the Lord.

Psalm 130:1–2, 3–4, 5–6ab, 6c–7, 8
Out of the depths, I cry to you, Lord.

Psalm 143:1–2, 5–6, 7ab and 8ab, 10
O Lord, hear my prayer.

Reading 2 from the New Testament
Select one of these readings for the second reading at your funeral liturgy. One of these readings may also be used at your Vigil reading instead of an Old Testament reading.

Romans 5:5–11
Since we are now justified by his blood, we will be saved through him from the wrath.

Romans 5:17–21
Where sin increased, grace overflowed all the more.

Romans 6:3–9 or 6:3–4, 8–9
We too might live in newness of life.

Romans 8:14–23
We also groan within ourselves as we wait for adoption, the redemption of our bodies.

Romans 8:31b–35, 37–39
What will separate us from the love of Christ?

Romans 14:7–9, 10c–12
Whether we live or die, we are the Lord's.

1 Corinthians 15:20–28 or 15:20–23
So too in Christ shall all be brought to life.

1 Corinthians 15:51–57
Death is swallowed up in victory.

2 Corinthians 4:14—5:1
What is seen is transitory, but what is unseen is eternal.

2 Corinthians 5:1, 6–10
We have a building from God, eternal in heaven.

Philippians 3:20–21
He will change our lowly bodies to conform to his glory.

Thessalonians 4:13–18
Thus we shall always be with the Lord.

2 Timothy 2:8–13
If we have died with him we shall also live with him.

1 John 3:1–2
We shall see him as he is.

1 John 3:14–16
We know that we have passed form death to life because we love our brothers.

Gospel Reading
Select one Gospel reading for your Vigil and one Gospel reading for your Funeral Liturgy.

Matthew 5:1–12a
Rejoice and be glad, for your reward will be great in heaven.

Matthew 11:25–30
Come to me and I will give you rest.

Matthew 25:1–13
Behold the bridegroom! Come out to him!

Matthew 25:31–46
Come, you who are blessed by my father.

Mark 15:33–39; 16:1–6 or 15:33–39
Jesus gave a loud cry and breathed his last.

Luke 7:11–17
Young man, I tell you, arise!

Luke 12:35–40
You also must be prepared.

Luke 23:33, 39–43
Today you will be with me in paradise.

Luke 23:44–46, 50, 52–53; 24:1–6a or 23:44–46, 50, 52–53
Father, into your hands I commend my spirit.

Luke 24:13–35 or 24:13–16, 28–35
Was it not necessary that the Christ should suffer these things and enter into his glory?

John 5:24–29
Whoever hears my word and believes has passed from death to life.

John 6:37–40
Everyone who sees the Son and believes in him may have eternal life and I shall raise him on the last day.

John 6:51–59
Whoever eats this bread will live forever, and I will raise them up on the last day.

John 11:17–27 or 11:21–27
I am the resurrection and the life.

John 11:32–45
Lazarus, come out!

John 12:23–28 or 12:23–26
If it dies, it produces much fruit.

John 14:1–6
In my Father's house there are many dwellings.

John 17:24–26
I wish that where I am they also may be with me.

John 19:17–18, 25–39
And bowing his head he handed over his spirit.

Funeral Music Suggestions

Music is an integral part of the Church's liturgy, and the funeral rites are liturgies of the Church. Any music selected for the funeral must be appropriate for Catholic worship. It should reflect on "the Lord's suffering, death, and triumph over death and should be related to the readings from Scripture"[2] and offer "a spirit of hope in Christ's victory over death and in the Christian's share in that victory."[3] Other types of music might be shared at another time, such as during the time of visitation or at a postfuneral meal. Most of the music for the funeral rites is already part of the parish musicians' repertoire. Choosing music that members of the parish already know will invite the mourners to participate in the singing.

Music ministers for funerals are usually those who already minister in the parish. The parish music director usually coordinates music and music ministers for funerals. At most funerals, an organist or pianist and a cantor from the parish are present. If additional musicians are desired, this should be coordinated by the music director. A list of common liturgical funeral music is provided below.

---

2. *Order of Christian Funerals*, 30.
3. *Order of Christian Funerals*, 31.

Popular Liturgical Songs

- "All Creatures of Our God and King" (traditional; various publishers)
- Alleluia! Sing to Jesus (traditional; various publishers)
- "Be Not Afraid" by Bob Dufford, SJ (OCP)
- "The Cloud's Veil" by Liam Lawton (GIA)
- "Come to Me" by J. Michael Joncas (GIA)
- "Eye Has Not Seen" by Marty Haugen (GIA)
- "For All the Saints" (Traditional; various publishers)
- "Go, Silent Friend" by John L. Bell (GIA)
- "God of Broken Hearts" by Zach Stachowski (GIA)
- "God Will Lead Us Home" by Chris de Silva (GIA)
- "Here I Am Lord" by Dan Schutte (OCP)
- "Hosea" by Gregory Norbet, OSB (OCP)
- "How Great Thou Art" (traditional; various publishers)
- "I Am the Bread of Life" by Suzanne Toolan, RSM (GIA)
- "I Am the Resurrection and the Life" by Bob Hurd (OCP)
- "I Have Loved You" by J. Michael Joncas
- "I Heard the Voice of Jesus Say" (traditional; various publishers)
- "I Know That My Redeemer Lives" by Howard Hughes, SM (GIA)
- "I Know That My Redeemer Lives" by Scott Soper (OCP)
- "Jerusalem, My Destiny" by Rory Cooney (GIA)
- "Jerusalem, My Happy Home" (traditional; various publishers)
- "Jesus, Remember Me" by Taizé (GIA)
- "The King of Love My Shepherd Is" (traditional; various publishers)
- "Lead Me Home" by Matt Maher (OCP)
- "Let Heaven Rejoice" by Bob Dufford, SJ (OCP)
- "Lord of All Hopefulness" (traditional; various publishers)
- "The Lord Will Heal the Broken Heart" by Liam Lawton (GIA)
- "Make Me a Channel of Your Peace" (traditional; various publishers)
- "May the Road Rise to Meet You" by Lori True (GIA)
- "On Eagle's Wings" by J. Michael Joncas (GIA)
- "Shepherd Me, O God" by Marty Haugen (GIA)
- "Sing with All the Saints in Glory" (traditional; various publishers)
- "Softly and Tenderly" (traditional; various publishers)
- "Ubi Caritas" by Taizé (GIA)
- "We Shall Rise Again" by Jeremy Young (GIA)
- "Ye Watchers and Ye Holy Ones" (traditional; various publishers)

CHAPTER SEVEN

Talking to Your Family about Death

*Our loved ones have not disappeared into dark nothingness:
Hope assures us that that they are in God's good and strong hands.
Love is stronger than death.*

—Pope Francis

After you complete working in this book, tell someone you trust about it. You may wish to discuss what you have written and what preparations you have made to be certain that it is clear. Much of the information found in this booklet contains sensitive material that could be subject to theft—be careful where this information is stored. There is information found in this booklet that will be helpful for your loved ones to know *before* your death such as end of life care. (Refer to the Letter to Readers on pages 1–3).

You might choose to use the letter on the following page to record this information. The page can then be removed from the book and given to the person to whom it is addressed or you may download a PDF of form letter on this website: www.LTP.org/HOUR3. However, it is best to engage in a personal conversation with the person that you would like to be responsible for ensuring that your last wishes are taken care of.

Since discussing death can be a very difficult and awkward conversation, here are some things to consider when approaching them about this topic. First, think about the person you've chosen and the task you are asking them to undertake.

- How do you think they will respond to your request of them? Will they be uncomfortable even talking to you about your death? Will they feel overwhelmed by the responsibility?

- What would make the conversation and the tasks more comfortable for them? For example, would it help for them to know that making these plans has given you a lot of peace and lightness of spirit? Would they be enriched to know that reading through the funeral rites and making your selections has reminded you that your life will be changed and not ended and that your faith in God's mercy and love has been strengthened? Would they feel closer to you and have a sense of purpose in knowing that you are entrusting them with something very important to you?
- Have you spoken together in the past about Catholic faith and last things, or will this be new? Do you share the same faith, or will you need to explain why the funeral rites are reassuring and powerful to you?
- How do you anticipate that other family members or significant others will receive your plans when your designate presents them? Discussing together how things might unfold would help your designate mentally prepare and avoid anxiety.
- What is your hope for the way your funeral will affect those who mourn you?
- Would it be helpful for you and your designate to pray together at the end of this conversation?

Sample discussion points to help begin the conversation:

- As you know, I prefer to think ahead and make preparations early. Although no one likes to talk about death, it is important for the family to know my wishes for my funeral and to be aware of my finances. By having these matters settled before I die, your burdens will be eased when that day comes. Instead of making hurried preparations, you will be able to consult this booklet. That should be calming for you and the rest of the family. All of you will be able to better embrace my leaving this transitory life to go to our home in heaven.
- I would like to present you with a gift. At this moment, you might not think of a booklet that provides the titles of the hymns and the citations of the readings at my funeral as a gift. And you may feel that it is too soon for me to indicate financial matters that you will need to know after my death. Discussing these matters is often put off for another day. But as Jesus tells his disciples in the Gospel of Luke, we need to be prepared. It is just as important to be vigilant in matters surrounding our death as it is in other areas of our life. With this information at hand, you will not be in a quandary about the hymns and readings at Mass but will know my preferences. Neither will you wonder if a bank account or a financial

matter has been overlooked. When the time comes for this information, you will understand why I call the preparation in this booklet a gift.

- I want to take a few moments to talk to you about a booklet that I have prepared. You might not want to think about the possibility of my dying, but it is a reality that we need to face. And, of course, the fact of our death is not as important as that eternal life awaits us. This booklet contains my wishes for my funeral as well as financial and legal information that you will need to know upon my death. I am making you aware of it now so that your burdens will be lessened when I die. With temporal matters taken care of, you will be able to concentrate on the spiritual when I die.

◈ LETTER TO LOVED ONES

Date:

Dear _____,

I would like to present you with a gift. I have filled out a booklet called *Now and at the Hour of Our Death* and have recorded my requests for medical treatment, finances, death, and the funeral liturgy. My wishes reflect my Catholic beliefs.

At this moment, you might not think of a booklet that provides the titles of the hymns and the citations of the readings at my funeral as a gift. And you may feel that it is too soon for me to indicate financial matters that you will need to know after my death. Discussing these matters is often put off for another day. But as Jesus tells his disciples in the Gospel of Luke, we need to be prepared. It is just as important to be vigilant in matters surrounding our death as it is in other areas of our life. With this information at hand, you will not be in a quandary about the hymns and readings at Mass but will know my preferences. Neither will you wonder if a bank account or a financial matter has been overlooked. When the time comes for this information, you will understand why I call the preparation in this booklet a gift.

> Come to me,
> all you who labor and
> are burdened,
> and I will give you rest.
> —Matthew 11:28

I keep the book in the following place:

_____
_____

At the time of my death, I ask that you use the information in this book to the extent possible. I do hope that the booklet will also help you find hope and faith in God during the difficult time of my passing.

With gratitude and love,

APPENDIX

Tasks for My Loved Ones

> Christian hope faces the reality of death and the anguish
> of grief but trusts confidently that the power of sin and death
> has been vanquished by the risen Lord.
> —*Order of Christian Funerals*, 8

This section is for family members to read upon news of your death. Obviously, they will need to know ahead of time that they should be using this booklet in order to take care of your wishes. They should read this section as a general check list of things that will need to be taken care of and prayed for. Many duties must be carried out and many decisions must be made at the time of death. This section will assist your survivors as they tend to the duties and decisions that will surround your funeral and burial. The topics are cross-referenced to pages in this booklet. This section is available on www.LTP.org/HOUR3. Give to your family members.

Prayers before Death and at the Time of Death

The Church gives us prayers for the moments before and following death and may be led by family members. Prayers are provided here for them to use.

When a person is near death, consider offering a reading from Scripture such as Psalm 23. You might follow the reading with the Litany of Saints. Your loved one has noted his or her favorite saint below.

My patron saint:

_____

This prayer may be said when the moment of death is near. Consider also singing a favorite hymn. Music is often comforting to those who are nearing death.

> I commend you, my dear brother/sister, to almighty God,
> and entrust you to your Creator.
> May you return to him
> who formed you from the dust of the earth.
> May holy Mary, the angels, and all the saints
> come to meet you as you go forth from this life.
> May Christ who was crucified for you
> bring you freedom and peace.
> May Christ who died for you
> admit you into his garden of paradise.
> May Christ, the true Shepherd,
> acknowledge you as one of his flock.
> May he forgive all your sins,
> and set you among those he has chosen.
> May you see your Redeemer face to face,
> and enjoy the vision of God for ever.
> **All:** Amen.[1]

The following prayer may be used at the time of death:

> Saints of God, come to his/her aid!
> Come to meet him/her angels of the Lord!
> **All:** Receive his/her soul and present him/her to God the Most Hight.
>
> May Christ, who called you, take you to himself;
> may angels lead you to Abraham's side.
> **All:** Receive his/her soul and present him/her to God the Most High.
>
> Give him/her eternal rest, O Lord, and may your light shine on him/her for ever.
> **All:** Receive his/her soul and present him/her to God the Most High.[2]

---

1. *Pastoral Care of the Sick: Rites of Anointing and Viaticum*, 220B.
2. *Pastoral Care of the Sick: Rites of Anointing and Viaticum*, 221.

Following the "Saints of God" the following prayer is offered by a family member.

> Let us pray (all pause for a moment of silence).
> All-powerful and merciful God,
> we commend to you **N.**, your servant.
> In your mercy and love,
> blot out the sins he/she has committed through human weakness.
> In this world he/she has died:
> let him/her live with you for ever.
> Through Christ our Lord.
> **All:** Amen.[3]

Tasks Immediately upon Death

When a loved one dies in the hospital, nursing home, assisted living or hospice facility, the medical staff or hospice nurse will help you with contacting the necessary people and declaring your loved one as deceased. They should be informed if you would like a priest to come before the body is removed from the facility. If death happens at home, especially suddenly, call 911. A medical professional will be needed to officially declare your loved one as deceased. Protocols may vary from state to state, especially if an autopsy is needed. The official declaration of death is needed before contacting the funeral home or memorial/cremation society. If you would like the parish priest to offer prayers over your loved one, before his or her body is taken from the home, he should be contacted immediately.

Preparation of the Body

While the body is being prepared for viewing, a family member may offer this prayer (of course, families might ask the funeral director or a parish priest to do this as well):

> Into your hands, O Lord,
> we humbly entrust our brother/sister **N.**
> In this life you embraced him/her with your tender love;
> deliver him/her now from every evil
> and bid him/her enter eternal rest.
> The old order has passed away:
> welcome him/her then into paradise,
> where there will be no sorrow, no weeping nor pain,

---

3. *Pastoral Care of the Sick: Rites of Anointing and Viaticum*, 221A.

> but the fullness of peace and joy
> with your Son and the Holy Spirit
> for ever and ever.
> **All:** Amen.[4]

Transferring the Body

The funeral home is responsible for transferring your loved one's body to the church for services and to the cemetery for burial. This may include the Vigil service at the wake, as some churches provide the option for people to be "waked" in the parish church. When the body is transferred, this prayer may accompany the body:

> **N.** is gone now from this earthly dwelling
> and has left behind those who mourn his/her absence.
> Grant that as we grieve for our brother/sister
> we may hold his/her memory dear
> and live in hope of the eternal Kingdom
> where you will bring us together again.
> Through Christ our Lord.
> **All:** Amen.[5]

Death Certificate

In the United States, the law requires that a death certificate be issued by the county in which a person dies. The death certificate must be signed by a doctor. If the deceased has been under a doctor's care or has died in a hospital, this is a routine and expected duty of the attending physician; although a hospice nurse is able to sign the certificate. If the deceased has died unexpectedly and in their home, call 911. They will advise you as to what needs to take place next; whether EMTs are sent to collect the body or the county coroner. Copies of the death certificate will be needed at a later date when filing insurance claims and probating the will, and for other legal matters. The funeral home will be able to help you with acquiring the death certificate. If your loved one was a veteran, they may be entitled to extra copies at no cost.

Wake (Vigil Service), Funeral Mass, and Burial

From the perspective of faith, the rites of the Church are the central actions surrounding death. The funeral liturgies are a sign of shared Christian faith and they

---

4. *Order of Christian Funerals*, 117B.
5. *Order of Christian Funerals*, 125.

provide consolation to those who mourn. Survivors meet with the priest or other pastoral minister from the parish of the deceased to prepare wake and funeral liturgies. Although the wake may take place in the funeral or memorial home, the Catholic service that takes place here is the responsibility of the Church, as are the funeral Mass (or service of the Word), and burial service. You should contact the parish immediately upon the death of your loved one to make these arrangements. (Refer to page chapters 3, 4, 5, and 6 regarding your loved one's plans for their funeral services.)

If your loved one has left no cemetery plans, a representative of a chosen cemetery will meet with the survivors and present various options. Some cemeteries limit the types and styles of grave markers according to the location of the grave and the number of graves purchased. Some require either a burial vault or a grave liner to enclose the coffin in the grave. Requirements and restrictions should be discussed before any purchase. Some cemeteries have grave sites and columbariums (places for the vessels holding ashes) set aside for cremated remains. Cremated remains may also be buried in a traditional grave. (Refer to chapter 4 regarding your loved one's plans for burial.)

Immediately after Burial

Many families share a meal together after the burial and extend an invitation to all who took part in the funeral liturgy. Sometimes the parish hall is used for this gathering; sometimes the family home or a hall or restaurant is used. Your survivors should know whether or not your parish is prepared to provide for such a gathering. Refer to page 51 for your loved one's plans.

In the Days after Burial

It is the executor's duty to file the will in court, usually within thirty days of death. If no will exists, survivors will need to consult an attorney to determine the proper procedure to be followed. A provision in most wills gives the executor power to pay funeral and burial costs from the estate of the deceased. If no previous arrangement has been made, survivors need to work with the executor of the will to purchase an appropriate burial marker.[6] Refer to pages 44–45 in chapter 4 regarding your loved one's plans for the memorial marker.

---

6. Both *Consumer Reports* and AARP provide helpful check lists for families to use for arrangements. Visit the following websites: https://www.aarp.org/home-family/friends-family/info-2020/when-loved-one-dies-checklist.html and https://www.consumerreports.org/family/what-to-do-when-a-loved-one-dies/.

Persons to Notify

Persons to notify of your death, especially those unlikely to see a death notice or those not well known by your immediate family:

Name	Telephone Number	Email Address